The Leader's Brain:

HOW ARE YOU USING THE OTHER 95%

DR. BASTIAAN HEEMSBERGEN

Printed in Victoria, Canada

A cataloguing record for this book that includes the U.S. Library of Congress Classification number, the Library of Congress Call number and the Dewey Decimal cataloguing code is available from the National Library of Canada. The complete cataloguing record can be obtained from the National Library's online database at: www.nlc-bnc.ca/amicus/index-e.html
ISBN: 1-4120-3027-7

TRAFFORD

This book was published on-demand in cooperation with Trafford Publishing. On-demand publishing is a unique process and service of making a book available for retail sale to the public taking advantage of on-demand manufacturing and Internet marketing. **On-demand publishing** includes promotions, retail sales, manufacturing, order fulfilment, accounting and collecting royalties on behalf of the author.

Suite 6E, 2333 Government St., Victoria, B.C. V8T 4P4, CANADA

Phone	250-383-6864	Toll-free	1-888-232-4444 (Canada & US)
Fax	250-383-6804	E-mail	sales@trafford.com
Web site	www.trafford.com	TRAFFORD PUBLISHING IS A DIVISION OF TRAFFORD HOLDINGS LTD.	
Trafford Catalogue #04-0854		www.trafford.com/robots/04-0854.html	

10   9   8   7   6   5   4   3   2

Inspired by the memory of my generous and kind father Ryk, the heroic compassion of my mother Tina, the courage of my sister Anne, and the friendship of my brother Adriaan.

A dedication to all who are affected by and who care for loved ones with Huntington's Chorea (HD).

TABLE OF CONTENTS

ACKNOWLEDGEMENTS i

INTRODUCTION:
YOUR EYE DOESN'T SEE AS MUCH AS YOU THINK ii

Why Read This Book Now? vii

Does the Brain Trick the Eye? viii

Blindspots of Leaders ix

Mindsets and the Nonaware Mind xi

CHAPTER ONE:
REDISCOVERING THE BRAIN 1

Did you Know? 2

The Decade of the Brain 3

Neuroplasticity: "You Can Teach Old Dogs New Tricks" 5

The Savant Brain: "Seeing the World Exactly as It Is" 7

Nonconscious Skills 8

The Brain Partitions 11

Here and Now Thinking 14

CHAPTER TWO:
THE NONCONSCIOUS BRAIN – HOW IMPORTANT IS IT? 15

Doing Without Thinking About It? 16

Reawakening The Brain: "Use It or Lose It"! 21

Nonconscious Problem Solving 23

CHAPTER THREE:
LEADERS, DROP YOUR MINDSETS AND TAP THE NONCONSCIOUS 27

Mental Models 29

Filtering Consciousness Through Paradigms 31

Paradigms: Mindsets and Patterns 32

Blueprints and Templates 35

You See More than Your Eye Does 36

Signal Detection Theory 37

The Selective Attention Task 38

Paradigm Shift 39

Drop the Old Paradigms When They Don't Fit Anymore 41

Functional Fixedness 42

How Do We Keep Up? 43

Pay Attention to Where You Pay Attention 43

CHAPTER FOUR:
LEADING WITH MINDFULNESS: TURNING OFF THE AUTOMATIC PILOT 45

Mindfulness 46

Conscious Processing 50

Language of Mindlessness 51

Why Mindfulness? 51

The Mindful Leader's Behaviours and Resulting Benefits 52

How Does Mindful Thinking Work? 56

How Often Are We Mindless? 59

The Beginner's Mind 60

CHAPTER FIVE:
FRESH PERCEPTION: ART AND LEADERSHIP, IS THERE A SYNERGY? 63

Making Unexpected Connections 64

Unfamiliar and Volatile Environments 66

Aesthetics and the Arts **67**

What Leaders Can Learn From Painters? **69**

Is Artful Leadership the Answer? **71**

Leonardo da Vinci **76**

CHAPTER SIX:
DEVELOPING THE LEADER'S DISCOVERY CAPACITY 79

The Blueprint and the Blank Canvas **80**

How Are You Painting Your Canvas? **81**

The Painted Canvas **82**

Blank Canvas Leadership **86**

Creating Restorative Mind Space **87**

What Helps Our Capacity to Voluntarily Attend? **89**

Develop a Curious Response **90**

Retreat and Reflect: Provide Opportunities for "Being Time" **93**

Slow Down Your Thinking: Theta Brain Waves **95**

Pay Attention and Notice: Situational Awareness (SA) **98**

Immerse Yourself **100**

Deep Situational Awareness: Framing **100**

What Is Deep Situational Understanding (DSU)? **101**

What Key Capacity Is Required to Enhance SA? **102**

Further Diagnostic Questions to Assess SA **105**

How Can Leaders Increase SA? **106**

Physical Space **109**

What Kinds of Physical Environments Have Restorative Potential? **110**

Summary of Creating Restorative Space **111**

CHAPTER SEVEN:
THE NEW LEADERSHIP SENSING TOOLBOX 113

Part One: Visual Practices for a New Leadership Era 114

The Visual Approach 114

Metaphors 115

Artistic Metaphors 117

Accessibility of Metaphors 117

Imaginization 118

Innovative Visualization - A Picture Is Worth a Thousand Words 119

What Types of Visual Tools Are Available to Leaders? 124

The Visual Toolkit - How Leaders Can Think Visually 125

      Mindscape 125

      The Cube 126

      Visual Explorer 127

      Drawing: Another Tool in the Doctor's Bag? 129

      If Words Aren't Enough, Show Me 130

      What is Concept Mapping? 133

      How Are Mind Maps Created? 133

      What Is Clustering? 135

      Zaltman Metaphor Elicitation Tool (ZMET) 135

I Can See Clearly Now the Brain Is Gone 136

CHAPTER EIGHT:
THE NEW LEADERSHIP SENSING TOOLBOX 139

Part Two: Movement and Sound Practices for a
New Leadership Era: 140

What Can Improvisation Teach Leaders? 140

What Is Improvisation? 141

What Can Sculptors Teach Leaders? 147

What Can Theatre Teach Leaders? 150

What Can Narrative Teach Leaders? 151

Listen With a Third Ear 155

What Can Music Teach Leaders? 156

Hearing and Expressing the Inner Voice of the Leader 158

AFTERWORD 159

APPENDIX:

Using Art in Developing Leadership 163

ENDNOTES 165

ACKNOWLEDGMENTS

I would like to thank my muse and former professor, Dr. J. P. Das; Colin Funk, a master weaver whose practice and mind have been informative and inspirational; and Henry Kutarna an extraordinary coach and mentor who provided unwavering support. I have also borrowed generously from conversations with my colleagues at the Banff Centre: Andre Mamprin, Kevin Yousie, Ed Bamiling, Kevin Asbjörnson, Jane Newman, and John Murrell. The editing of Kirsten Craven and the layout and design by Laurie Buxton have made my tome more palatable, succinct, and colourful. I would also like to thank Myra Cridland my confidant, encourager, and life partner. I am so grateful for her comments on earlier drafts of this book; her patience with my tedious nonconscious ramblings regarding its content, and her steadfast support. Luke, my dearest son, has fostered the explorer in me and taught me to look with fresh eyes and expanded categories.

To all of you I would like to express my deep and profound gratitude.

INTRODUCTION: YOUR EYE DOESN'T SEE AS MUCH AS YOU THINK

Seeing stars, it dreams of eternity. Hearing birds, it makes music. Smelling flowers, it is enraptured. Touching tools, it transforms the earth. But deprived of these sensory experiences, the human brain withers and dies.[1]

Ronald Kotulak

Neuroscientists have uncovered much of what we know about the brain during the last ten years, also known as the Brain Decade.[2] The most important discovery to emerge in the last five years is that the human brain is more changeable than we ever thought.[3] Even in adulthood, some areas of the brain can renew themselves, producing new nerve cells.[4] The brain can also rewire itself in response to experience. This is an astonishing finding since "for most of its 100-year history, neuroscience has strongly held a central belief: a mature adult's brain remains a stable, unchanging, computer like machine with fixed memory and processing power. You can lose brain cells, the story has gone, but you certainly cannot gain new ones."[5] Apparently the axiom, "You can't teach old dogs new tricks", has now been refuted.

Neuroscience research now supports the idea that we can learn new tricks throughout our lifetimes. The ability of the brain to change through the process of learning is what is known as *neuroplasticity.* So how does the brain change? According to Daniel Drubach, there appears to be at least two types of modifications that occur in the brain with learning: change in the internal structure of the neurons, the most notable being in the area of synapses, and an increase in the number of synapses between neurons.[6] The corollary of teaching old dogs new tricks is also of course the idea of "use it or lose it."

This brain research can significantly inform the practice of leadership. Of particular interest to me is the subject of cognition, or how leaders think and how they can enhance their brain capability. This book is about making unexpected connections between brain research and our knowledge of the nonconscious, leadership development, the artistic process, and how people think. Making these connections will provide new processes and tools to support leaders who face a volatile, unpredictable, and information-rich environment.

My own interest in cognition and how to improve our thinking to enable the production and implementation of new leadership ideas began when I was an educational psychology student at the University of Alberta. I was fascinated by experiments involving neurological and cognitive structures – in particular, how people think. I was especially interested in the theory of frontal lobe functioning and metacognition, or how we think about our thinking. While looking for a topic for my doctoral research, a professor named Dr. J. P. Das invited me to explore the works of a Russian neuroscientist Alexander Luria, and to begin a process of researching frontal lobe functions. Shortly after, I was hooked. Since that time I have been intrigued by the difference between my graduate scientific self and my personal self. In my personal life, I visit art galleries, listen to and play the piano, and am proud of the poetry and visual artworks I produce. It is only in the last year that these seemingly disparate selves have come together, which explains the creation of this book.

As a faculty member at the Banff Centre in Alberta, Canada, a centre for creative and innovative excellence, I work with and am constantly in the presence of artists. Over the past year, our team leadership development at the Banff Centre has been exploring the link between leadership development and art.

I am fortunate in being able to pursue my passion for understanding how our knowing and thinking as individuals, teams, organizations, and societies can shape and deal with today's complex world. Building on research from diverse disciplines like neurology, sociology, cognitive science, and psychology, I have been trying to understand how humans think and become more effective as leaders.

Is there a systematic way to unleash fresh leadership thinking and novel solutions using recent brain research and knowledge from the world of art? What if leaders could:

see what's coming with fewer surprises and avoid inattentional blindness?

make the brain and mind work more effectively?

probe beneath the surface to reveal "what they don't know they know"?

understand what customers and employees are thinking more accurately?

see things as they really are without bias or assumption?

see the raw data of the world as it is, actually represented in the nonconscious mind?

unlock the images that lie within the brain?

experience differences in thought processes as they occur in the brain?

interfere with the way the brain works and stop it from analyzing and editing information?

change the brain's operating system rather than rewiring it?

plunge in and out of the conscious mind at will?

switch parts of the brain and turn on other parts at will?

use mental exercises to learn how to suppress some areas of the brain, while tapping into and developing any hidden potential?

Robert Frost once said, "The mind is a wonderful organ – it starts working the moment you get up in the morning and does not stop until you get to the office." This book is designed to improve your ability to lead yourself and others in dynamic and sometimes unpredictable environments. In these environments, leaders need to access their untapped cognitive potential and improve their ability to think accurately and imaginatively. Today's leaders need a set of skills and tools to help them detect signals, embrace uncertainty, exploit opportunities for change, and respond appropriately in the moment, at the top of their intelligence.

There are currently many extremely useful tools for leaders using conceptual learning that are anchored in management and behavioural science. However, reason and analysis by themselves are no longer sufficient. To truly thrive in the midst of uncertainty, volatility, and complexity, leaders must act calmly and decisively in real-time, skills that can only be acquired through accessing a new set of tools anchored in brain research and the world of the arts or aesthetics. This book will teach leaders how to thrive in dynamic environments and equip them with capacities to maximize their potential as leaders.

The French novelist Marcel Proust said, "The real voyage of discovery consists not in seeking new landscapes, but in having new eyes."[7] The premise of this book is the belief that many barriers to effective leadership can be removed by engaging the mind in new perceptions, exercising our brain and our thinking, and bypassing the mind's conceptual thinking and gaining conscious access to the raw uninterrupted information of our basic perceptions. In so doing, leaders can improve their capacity to sense, tune in, identify, and respond to emerging opportunities. They can also become more effective in dealing with and responding to complexity, volatility, and change, and avoid missing critical signals requiring different mindsets.

WHY READ THIS BOOK NOW?

We live in a period of complexity, chaos, and discontinuous change. We are now facing a world where surprise and uncertainty are the dominant themes. It is a world that is much more unpredictable and challenging than it used to be. The instability of the economy, terrorism, new epidemics, the acceleration of technological change, and the recent surge of unethical business practices have given rise to a climate that demands:

seeing clearly and detecting the signals that need attention and responsiveness;

cleaning out our lenses, widening our lenses, imaging new futures, and thinking differently, using the brain more effectively;

moving beyond simple left-brain/right-brain theories.

Yet leaders frequently fail to see what, in hindsight, were some clear signals that would assist them in responding appropriately. The world is becoming more turbulent faster than most leaders are becoming more resilient. Why?

DOES THE BRAIN TRICK THE EYE?

Karl Weick, a noted management researcher from the University of Michigan, suggests that the eye does not see as much as one thinks, because leaders tend to "see what they believe," rather than "believe what they see."[8] The result is inattentional blindness, a lack of awareness in detecting signal changes as they occur. Why is this so? Most people assume that what you see is pretty much what your eye sees and reports to your brain. In other words, "I believe what eye believes."[9] In fact, you see more than your eye does.

Your brain adds very substantially to the report it gets from your eye, so that a lot of what you see is actually "made up" by the brain. Therefore, what is probably more accurate is "eye believes what I believe."[10] We see the world through our own lenses or mindsets. Our rules and regulations about the world act as filters for what we see. Data and information that agrees with our mindset has an easy path and is easily seen. However, data that does not agree with our mindset is usually distorted to fit our mindset, rejected or denied as relevant.

We only select data that fits our mindset for how things are supposed to be. Humans, as individuals and groups, frequently deny the relevance of information they don't want to deal with. We can therefore be blinded by what we know. We can be blinded by our expertise, our mindsets, filters, paradigms, beliefs, orthodoxies, and rules of engagement, many of which we are not conscious or aware of. We are blind to what *we don't know we don't know.* We can be so focused on the goal or the outcome that we don't pay attention to what is going on right in front of us. Such an orientation sometimes makes us miss our present experience. It also creates a debilitating attachment to the outcome.

BLINDSPOTS OF LEADERS
PICTURE THIS:

- An employee/team member/ manager may receive data about their behaviour from 360-degree feedback. The feedback indicates that the individual in question has engaged in micromanagement behaviour, which they are not conscious or aware of. The individuals lens or mindset in discussions indicates a belief that "if you want a job done right, you have to do it yourself." They have developed a blindspot making them unaware of their behaviour and therefore reluctant to change this behaviour. Their mindset of "how to get things done" prevented them from seeing new data.

■ A manager promotes a team member whose performance continues to be below average in results and leadership capacity. The manager receives feedback from colleagues questioning the validity of the promotion. The manager defends the promotion on the basis of the specific industry knowledge possessed by the team member, *unaware* of the impact on team performance and deliverables. The manager's *mindset* reduced their capacity to see new data that suggested an inappropriate decision.

■ An airline finds itself in serious financial difficulty with significant financial losses in successive years, their executives unaware of new customer and market data. Executives from a new entrant airline notice the new data and customer signals requiring change and replace the *old mindset* of, passengers are "bums in seats," with "customers need to be aggressively wooed through service." Likewise the new entrant executives replace the mindset that "the long haul route is the important segment and commuter traffic is incidental," with "commuters are an important segment all their own."

In all of the above examples, leaders, managers and team members had blindspots which resulted in negative consequences. The responses to these consequences are usually met with statements of surprise and incredulity. "I didn't see it coming," or

"I think I'm still in shock because it was pretty out of the blue," or "I knew things were tough, I never thought this was going to happen." Is it possible to extricate ourselves from surprise and unawareness? Can we access the unprocessed raw information about the world and see the world the way it really is without putting our own filters or mindsets on it? Can we be a blank canvas without projecting what we think? Just think of the rich applications if we could actually do all of these things.

Our mindsets are not to be discarded as useless. We need our mindsets to operate automatically in familiar situations. According to estimates, we make between three and thirty thousand decisions each day.[11] It would be too difficult and challenging if we had to make each and every decision without the assistance of our mindset (how to talk, how to breathe, how to eat and so on). However, in unfamiliar, unpredictable, complex, and volatile situations we need to look with fresh eyes and adopt new mindsets. The challenge for leaders is to go beyond their current ways of thinking and their mindsets in order to see things differently, to not miss the signals. Leaders need to see what is truly there. Unfortunately what is truly there is not always available in our conscious (aware) mind as the previous examples illustrate. Fortunately, the world of aesthetics and art provides the tools and processes to uncover what is there.

MINDSETS AND THE NONAWARE MIND

The (nonaware) mind is very powerful. What is important to note here is that the nonconscious represents 95 percent of our thinking.[12] It is the executive centre of the brain; it controls most of our thinking. The nonconscious brain takes in everything we see, hear, touch, taste, and smell. It also stores our memories, past experiences, and mindsets. The cure for inattentional blindness is to access the information contained in the nonconscious brain; it is the ability to create or adopt new categories, to receive and accept new information, to adopt a different or additional perspective. Children do all these things naturally and easily. But these processes sometimes deteriorate as we grow older.

Who should read this book? The answer is people, who at all levels, are called upon to act quickly and innovatively to unanticipated changes in their environment.

1

CHAPTER ONE:
REDISCOVERING THE BRAIN

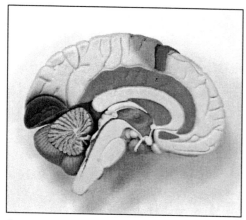

Figure 1-1: The human brain

How can leaders use the growing body of research on how the brain and the mind make sense of our world to become more effective? Cognitive neuroscientists have gained greater insights into how the brain interacts with and learns from its environment. So the relevant question becomes: What do we know about brain functioning and how can this knowledge be used to develop practical guidelines for leadership?

DID YOU KNOW?

■ Ninety percent of what we know about the brain has been learned in the past ten years.[1]

■ More than 34,000 research papers about the brain are published each year. [2]

■ Ninety-five percent of our brain is not used in logical conscious thinking.[3]

- If all the neurons in our brain were lined up side by side they would stretch one thousand kilometres. However the line would be only ten microns wide - invisible to the naked eye.[4]

- We have roughly twenty billion neocortical cells in our brain.[5]

- The brain can rewire itself in response to experience (plasticity).[6]

- All of our brain and its associated resources are constantly in use.[7]

THE DECADE OF THE BRAIN

During the 1990s, neuroscientists learned a great deal. The decade is referred to as the "decade of the brain," during which more was learned about this organ than during the entire previous history of neuroscience and psychology.[8] If 90 percent of what we know about the brain has been learned in the past ten years, it is time that we as leaders move past simple right-brain/left-brain theories to embrace new ideas to meet the challenges of today.

The resurgence of research, knowledge and writing are due to the maturity of the sciences of the brain and mind. There are now new techniques that permit the effective study of the neural substrates of mind processing, which have helped to produce new findings. In parallel, there are new theoretical developments, which have been prompted by the new findings. This combination allows for effective formulation and testing of hypotheses.

Recent technology has enabled neuroscientists to see inside the living brain. These brain-imaging methods help neuroscientists to understand the relationships between specific areas of the brain and what function they serve, locate the areas of the brain that are affected by neurological disorders, and develop new strategies to treat brain disorders.[9] The four main brain-imaging techniques are Electrophysiological recordings (EEG), Magneto-encephalography (MEG), Positron Emission Tomography (PET), Functional Magnetic Resonance Imaging (fMRI). The EEG traces brain electrical activity in response to a specific external stimulus. Electrodes are placed on specific parts of the brain, depending on which sensory system is being tested, to make recordings that are then processed by a computer.[10] Magneto-encephalography (MEG) one of the latest advances in scanners, reveals the source of weak magnetic fields emitted by neurons. An array of cylinder-shaped sensors monitors the magnetic field pattern near the patient's head to determine the positions and strengths of activity in various regions of the brain. In contrast with other imaging techniques, the MEG can characterize rapidly changing patterns of neural activity with millisecond resolution, and provide a quantitative measure of its strength for individual subjects.[11] PET is a method of measuring brain function that is based on the detection of radioactivity emitted when positrons, positively charged particles, undergo radioactive decay in the brain. The PET projects images detecting blood flow, as well as metabolic and chemical activity in the brain.[12] Finally, the fMRI is a technique that measures brain activity under resting and activated conditions.

The fMRI is an exciting new development. It combines the high spatial resolution and noninvasive imaging of brain anatomy offered by the standard MRI with a strategy for detecting changes in blood oxygenation levels driven by neuronal activity. This technique allows for the creation of more detailed maps of brain areas underlying human mental activities in health and disease. To date, the fMRI has been applied to the study of various functions of the brain ranging from primary sensory responses to cognitive activities.[13] Although the human brain is immensely complicated, we have known for some time that it carries out four basic functions: getting information (sensory cortex), making meaning of information (back integrative cortex), creating new ideas from these meanings (front integrative cortex) and acting on those ideas (motor cortex).[14]

NEUROPLASTICITY:
"YOU CAN TEACH OLD DOGS NEW TRICKS"

What is brain plasticity? *Plasticity*, or *neuroplasticity* is the lifelong ability of the brain to reorganize neural pathways based on new experiences.[15] As we learn, we acquire new knowledge and skills through instruction or experience. In order to learn or memorize a fact or skill, there must be persistent functional changes in the brain that represent the new knowledge. The ability of the brain to change with learning is what is known as *neuroplasticity*. In order to illustrate plasticity, imagine making an impression of a coin in a lump of clay. In order for the impression of the coin to appear in the clay, the shape of the clay changes as the coin is pressed into the clay. Similarly, the neural circuitry in the brain must reorganize in response to experience or sensory stimulation.

Research findings on neuroplasticity refute the axiom, "You can't teach old dogs new tricks." In fact, leaders can learn new tricks throughout their lifetimes. The key is continuing to seek out new experiences and to reflect on their meaning in light of what we already know. Leaders can also learn how to become refined sensors, to collect subtle cues by "sniffing out signals in the environment and sensing what's going on without having anything spelled out for them."[16] Instead of reflexively asking, "How do you feel?" leaders will increasingly try to find out how internal and external customers perceive the world. They'll find out more not only about how clients feel, but how they fear, see, and even smell things. They'll tune into their customers movement habits and other aspects of their behaviour that show how their brains work and how to communicate with them.[17]

There may have been a breakthrough in the way we understand the limits of our own intelligence and the functioning of the human brain in general. This breakthrough may in part be due to the research of Alan Snyder, director of the Centre for the Mind in Sydney, Australia; Dr. Gerald Zaltman, a marketing professor from Harvard; and Dr. Bruce Miller, a dementia specialist at the University of California at San Francisco. Snyder in particular thinks he has identified the part of the brain, which if switched off, can stimulate leadership breakthroughs. By temporarily inhibiting neural activity through a technique called *transcranial magnetic stimulation* (TMS), Snyder has discovered new insights into how we can improve a leader's thinking capability.[18]

TMS is used to inhibit or activate different regions of an individual's brain. While the stimulus is applied, the individual's skills and behaviour are tested in different areas that require cognitive processing. This reveals what cognitive effects the stimulation is having on the person. Amazingly, preliminary studies indicate that by using this technique, savant skills (a condition made famous by Dustin Hoffman in the Oscar-winning film *Rain Man*) can be switched on in the person undergoing TMS.

In "Savant for a Day," New York Times reporter Lawrence Osborne reports drawing a picture of a dog four times at different stages of his exposure to (TMS) and showing improved results.[19] Researchers have also completed a study of "savant syndrome" in which people with severe mental disorders can exhibit extraordinary talents in the field of art, music, or mathematics.[20] The study found that healthy volunteers showed similar talents when parts of their brains were temporarily disabled. How can we tap into these abilities without the use of TMS and what does all this have to do with leadership development?

THE SAVANT BRAIN:
"SEEING THE WORLD EXACTLY AS IT IS"

Savants can't recognize faces, but they can draw like Leonardo da Vinci, and perform music and amazing mathematical feats despite their brain damage. As mentioned previously in the 1989 movie *Rain Man*, Dustin Hoffman accurately and sensitively portrays Raymond, an autistic savant with brilliant mathematical skills and significantly increased public awareness. In 2002, the British Broadcasting Corporation (BBC) also aired a program on savant syndrome entitled, "Fragments of Genius." One segment featured a man named Stephen Wiltshire, who was taken up in a helicopter over London and hours later produced a detailed and accurate drawing of a four square mile area of the city.[21]

Autistic savants brains function differently. Savants have profound intellectual disabilities. They have difficulty relating to and communicating with others and yet have a "fragment of genius" – astonishing abilities or talents in music, art, and mathematics.[22] They have acquired these talents without training and apparently the skill comes from within. Savants also have a prodigious memory. Only about 10% of people with autistic disorders have some savant skills and there are thought to be no more than twenty-five in the world.[23] These are rare individuals who, although severely brain damaged, display extraordinary skills - often in areas traditionally believed to be the preserve of the gifted intellect.[24]

NONCONSCIOUS SKILLS:
ONLY SAVANTS SEE THE WORLD AS IT REALLY IS

Preschool children draw, not so much what they see, but from previous images they have seen.[25] The drawing of a horse in figure 1-2, is fairly typical of a four year old.

Figure 1-2: Representative drawings of normal children, each at age four years and two months. (Emma and Teneal, Parents on Campus Preschool, Australian National University).[26]

However, as a five-year-old child, an autistic artist named Nadia could draw with the detailed perspective normally associated with the classical masters. Here is Nadia's drawing of a horse which looks very similar to some of Leonardo's best sketches.

Figure 1-3: Nadia's drawing of a horse.[27]

However, Nadia could not recognize her parents or describe what she was drawing. Researchers have been unable to explain why people have these talents. Two scientists have recently identified an area of the brain which they think may hold the key – the front temporal lobe. Dr. Bruce Miller has found that some of his patients with dementia were developing artistic talents. After scanning their brains, he found they all had problems in the same part of the brain – the left arterial temporal lobe.[28]

Why do savants and some dementia patients have these remarkable talents when they are so severely disabled in other ways? Allan Snyder's theory is that because a specific part of the brain does not work properly, abilities in another area may be unlocked. He says the savants have their gifts because of this "malfunction" of the brain, not in spite of it.[29] Snyder says, "They are exceptional in that they can tap in and somehow we can't. They have privileged access."[30] In savants, the top layer of mental processing – conceptual thinking, making conclusions – is somehow stripped away:[31] "Autistic children seem to be innately aware of shape from shading and other details that we suppress in order to instantly identify an object."[32] Snyder says the average person may have these skills but in order to access them, we need to learn to focus in a specific way.[33] He also believes that savants can lose these skills as they acquire language abilities, since these abilities trigger the development of a part of the analytical part of the brain which dominates in most people. Experts on autism say there are many theories about savants. For example, some experts believe that parts of their brain have become highly developed, but in isolation so that no connections are made.

THE BRAIN PARTITIONS

We all receive enormous amounts of information, which is then filtered dramatically. However, savants apparently miss the filtering stage of processing and retain all the information they receive. Savants are like infants in that they haven't yet formed concepts, so they see the world the way it is – with little meaning. Savants merely copy what they see. They don't filter information, which means they are unable to put it into neat packages called concepts.[34] If we were to lack the ability to conceptualize, then we would be more savant-like. Alternatively, if we block the conceptualization of what we see or sense, then we do see things the way they are – devoid of meaning.

Like other savant artists, Stephen Wiltshire's drawings depict exactly what he sees without embellishment, stylization, or interpretation. He makes no notes; impressions are indelibly and faithfully inscribed from a single exposure for later recall, and he draws swiftly, beginning anywhere on the page. Thus, like other savant artists Alonzo Clemons and Richard Wawro, his remarkable artistic ability is linked to an equally remarkable memory.[35]

If the damaged areas of the brain could be restored, the savant skill may also disappear, as was the case with Nadia, who drew extraordinarily well at ages three and four but lost that ability when she began to speak and conceptualize. Savants tap raw information they actually see on the retina before visual processing takes place. Savants develop an ability to draw in childhood. Similarly, musical savants have perfect pitch as they have access to a sensory level of auditory processing.[36] They appear to hear the world exactly as it is. Snyder believes autistic savants have access to very fast early brain processing; the nonconscious skills that calculate; the trajectory of a softball without the batter being aware of it. This explains how a severely mentally retarded five-year-old child can draw like Leonardo da Vinci without any training. Her skill is a form of mimicry.

Snyder's theory began with art, but he came to believe that all savant skills, whether in music, calculation, math, or spatial relationships, derive from a lightning-fast processor in the brain that divides things – time, space, or an object – into equal parts.[38] Dividing time might allow a savant child to know the exact time when they are awakened, and it might help another savant find the sweet spot in sounds by allowing them to sense millisecond differences in the sounds hitting the right and left ears. Splitting numbers might allow math savants to factor ten digit numbers or easily identify large prime numbers – which are impossible to split.

Miller has seen similar transformations in patients with frontotemporal dementia, a degenerative brain disease that strikes people in their fifties and sixties. Some of these patients, he says, spontaneously develop both interest and skill in art and music. Brain-imaging studies have shown that most patients with frontotemporal dementia who develop skills have abnormally low blood flow or low metabolic activity in their left temporal lobe.[39] These people gradually lose the ability to speak, read, and write, and also lose the ability to recognize faces. However, visual and spatial processing is better preserved. And guess what happens? Some of these patients suddenly start producing the most amazingly beautiful paintings and drawings, even though they had never had any artistic talent before the onset of their dementia.

The patients "really do lose the linguistic meaning of things," says Miller, who believes Snyder's ideas about latent abilities complement his own observations about frontotemporal dementia. "There's a loss of higher-order processing that goes on in the anterior temporal lobe." In particular, frontotemporal dementia damages the ventral stream, a region of the brain that is associated with naming objects.[40] Patients with damage in this area can't name what they're looking at, but they can often paint it beautifully. Miller has also seen physiological similarities in the brains of autistic savants and patients with frontotemporal dementia. When he performed brain-imaging studies on an autistic savant artist who started drawing horses at eighteen months, he saw abnormalities similar to those of artists with frontotemporal dementia: decreased blood flow and slowed neuronal firing in the left temporal lobe.[41]

Similarly, art savants typically begin drawings with minor features rather than overall outlines, suggesting that they tend to perceive individual details more prominently than the whole – or the concept – of what is drawn. Autistic children differ from nonautistic children in another way. Normal kids find it frustrating to copy a picture containing a visual illusion, such as M. C. Escher's drawing in which water flows uphill.[42] Autistic savant children don't. This fits into Snyder's idea that they're recording what they see without interpretation and reproducing it with ease in their own drawings.

If savants process and reproduce exactly what they see and hear, and if this processing takes place at the nonconscious level, what if we were all able to access the nonconscious? What would we be capable of? The feats of a savant? What role does the nonconscious play in the mind of the leader? According to Snyder, it might be possible to train someone to access this nonconscious state by controlling their brain waves.[43] How?

HERE AND NOW THINKING

We can access the nonconscious (the capacity demonstrated by savants) by keeping our mind deliberately at a level of what is called *bare attention*, which involves a detached observation of what is happening within us and around us in the present moment. In this practice, the mind is trained to remain in the present; open, quiet, and alert, contemplating the present event. All judgments and interpretations are suspended, or if they occur, are merely registered and then dropped. The savant simply notes whatever comes up just as it is occurring, riding the changes of events in the way a surfer rides the waves on the sea. The savant mind stays in the present, stands in the here and now, without getting swept away by the tides of distracting thoughts, thereby accessing the nonconscious.

To stimulate discussion and action, findings are presented with the aim of strengthening the leader's conviction that emerging leadership models are possible, even necessary; that leadership is a dynamic, ongoing, and never-ending process; and that most people can be active partners - both along the lines outlined in this book and, undoubtedly, in new and even more innovative ways. The answers can all be found in your brain.

2

CHAPTER TWO:
THE NONCONSCIOUS BRAIN –
HOW IMPORTANT IS IT?

Figure 2-1: The nonconscious mind below the surface.

DOING WITHOUT THINKING ABOUT IT?

Antonio Damasio, a prominent neuropsychologist has stated, "the brain knows more than the conscious mind reveals."[1] An iceberg can serve as a useful metaphor to understand the nonconscious mind and how it can work more cooperatively with the conscious mind. As the iceberg floats in the water, the huge mass of it remains below the surface. Only a small percentage of the whole structure is visible above the surface. In this way, the iceberg is like the mind. The conscious mind is what we notice above the surface, while the nonconscious mind, the largest and most powerful part, remains unseen below the surface.

No model of how the mind works disputes the tremendous power churning below the tip of the iceberg. Nonconscious resources are constantly supporting the conscious mind. Just think of all the things you know. If you drive, you use over thirty specific skills without being aware of them.[2] These are skills, not facts; they are processes requiring intelligence, decision-making, and training. These learned resources, which operate below the surface, are critical natural resources. The nonconscious mind regulates all the systems of the body and keeps them in harmony with each other.

The conscious mind, like the part of the iceberg above the surface, is a small portion of the whole being. The conscious mind is what we ordinarily think of when we say "my mind." It's associated with thinking, analyzing, and making judgments and decisions. It is also associated with looking and listening and feeling. The conscious mind is actively sorting and filtering its perceptions because only so much information can reside in consciousness at once. Only seven bits of information, plus or minus two can be held consciously at one time.[3] Everything else we are thinking, feeling, or perceiving right now, along with all of our memories, remains nonconscious until they are called into consciousness or until they rise spontaneously. The nonconscious mind is continually processing the various sensory inputs stored in short-term and long-term memory. Using your nonconscious to solve problems is a process of listening and a readiness to record ideas as they percolate into your conscious mind.

A recent discovery by two neurophysiologists, Benjamin Libet and Bertram Feinstein at Mount Zion Hospital in San Francisco, brings to light the interrelationship between our conscious and nonconscious mind.[4] By measuring the time it took for a touch stimulus on a patient's skin to reach the brain as an electrical signal, the researchers were able to demonstrate that the patient's decision to respond was based on the patient's nonconscious mind. What was even more surprising was that the patient was unaware that their nonconscious mind had already caused them to push the button before they had consciously decided to do so.

A major theme of this book is that much of the leader's thinking is nonconscious, beneath conscious awareness. Consciousness comes later, both in evolution and also in the way the brain processes information, and many judgments have already been determined before they reach consciousness. Most of our epiphanies and "eurekas" and important decision-making moments come from the nonconscious part of the brain. Possibly nothing we do, no action we take, and no feeling we have, is purely conscious. The nonconscious may in fact be the executive centre of the brain.

Let's call the nonconscious autonomic brain simply "the brain"; it's attached directly to the senses. The conscious aware portion of our gray matter we'll call the "mind." The brain gets sensations first. The five major sensory systems (vision, olfaction, audition, sensation, and gustation) not only process separate sensory modalities, but also extensively interact with and influence each other. The conscious mind rejects most of this sensory input and makes basic decisions about what to do next.

Leaders make up their minds, or rather, their brains make up their minds for them. The brain's interpreter spins yarns the way you do when recounting a dream. A lot more of the brain comes with "factory-installed" mechanics than we like to think. Yet, we are not aware of how we form our thoughts or how we articulate them. We are not aware of the mechanisms of vision, touch, smell, taste, or hearing. Much of our expertise is executed nonconsciously. Most of the time, our brain performs operations of which we are completely unaware, and by mechanisms, which are largely unknown to us in order to help us arrive at our final judgments.

When it comes to thinking about our customers, we leaders generally think we understand. We read their answers on market research forms and view them in focus groups through one-way mirrors. When they say they are "satisfied" or "very satisfied" on survey questionnaires, we accept their comments at face value and move forward to respond to their stated needs. Yet after all this research they still frequently leave us and go to our competitors. How does this happen?

According to Harvard Business School professor Dr. Gerald Zaltman's research which is described in his book, *How Customers Think*, people make up their minds based on the thoughts and feelings that lie below conscious awareness.[5] These feelings are built from a collection of clues the customer gathered together based on the emotional impressions they had of their interaction with the company, rather than on any single factor. Customers aren't conscious of their real feelings about products and purchases, yet their choices are governed by their nonconscious thoughts. A considerable amount of data indicates that as compared to consciously controlled cognition, the nonconscious information-acquisition processes are not only much faster, but are also more structurally sophisticated in the sense that they are capable of efficient processing of multidimensional and interactive relations between variables.

Nonconscious processing appears to be the real engine room of the mind, the real executive in charge. As such, it deserves further inquiry. We could be in for some genuine surprises if we had a better understanding of the mechanisms and the intent of the nonconscious brain. Even when constrained within our present human design, many of our major decisions are strongly influenced by nonconscious processing. Many of our methods for accessing experience focus on conscious reactions but fail to access the rich mine of the nonconscious, where our deepest desires, preferences, and emotions dwell. Such traditional methods are, in Zaltman's words, "verbocentric," that is, they are word-based.[6] There's an elementary but surprising flaw in using verbocentric methods: *humans think in images, not words.* Thoughts occur as images. Two-thirds of all stimuli reaching the brain are visual, with the balance being conveyed through sound, taste, smell, and touch.[7]

Words do, as Zaltman notes, play a key role in conveying our thoughts, *but they are not what constitute our thoughts.*[8] Brain scans have demonstrated that certain areas of the brain become active before our conscious awareness of a thought, and it is only later, when a person nonconsciously chooses to frame a thought in language, that areas of the brain associated with verbal language become active. When leaders do not tap into this dormant part of the brain they may be prone to missing key signs in the environment. Consequently new opportunities may be bypassed and potentially lost.

Our nonconscious brain can "see" things we are not currently thinking about or looking at in our conscious level of thought. In other words, when we are thinking of one thing (maybe listening to a song or changing stations on the car radio) our nonconscious neurons (brain) are seeing many other things at the same time. If any of these other things are important to us, the nonconscious will automatically send this message to our conscious thought level. This will occur no matter what we are thinking about at the time on our conscious level and no matter whether what we are thinking about is extremely important or not. For example, when driving a car, we don't have to be thinking about keeping the car between the white lines all the time to do so. It happens at our nonconscious level during most of the trip. Whatever is important to the leader, whatever the nonconscious brain neurons establish as critical or important, this will be sent to the level of consciousness every time anything related to that appears, no matter what else the leader is thinking of consciously at the time.

REAWAKENING THE BRAIN: "USE IT OR LOSE IT"

Can we access and enhance processes in our own nonconscious mind? Can we unveil the process and strategy of nonconscious brain processing and develop scientific ways to make them accessible?

The answer to the above questions, according to Snyder, is yes. TMS, or the "thinking cap", is used to inhibit or activate different regions of a person's brain.[9] While the stimulus is applied, the individual's skills and behaviour are tested in different areas require cognitive processing. Some researchers believe that an improvement in savant-like skills indicates that the individual has heightened access to their nonconscious brain mechanisms and that studying brain maps taken before and after the stimulation using an EEG can identify these.[10]

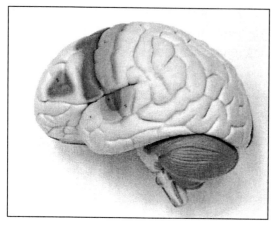

Figure 2-2: View of the left and anterior brain

Robyn Young and her colleague Michael Ridding at the University of Adelaide in Australia have used TMS on seventeen volunteers to inhibit their neural activity in the frontotemporal area.[11] This language and concept-supporting region of the brain is affected both in patients with frontotemporal dementia and savants. In this altered state, the volunteers were asked to perform savant – like tasks – drawing, calculating, and multiplying. Five of the seventeen volunteers improved their level of skill in doing these tasks, not to savant levels, but the researchers did not expect any improvement since savants do practice. While TMS isn't a precise tool for targeting regions of the brain, the five volunteers who improved in their tasks were those in whom separate neurological assessments indicated that the frontotemporal area was successfully targeted. Commenting on the plausibility of inhibiting brain regions and stimulating performance, Young says, "obviously I don't think the idea is so outlandish anymore", commented Young. "I think it is a plausible hypothesis. It always was, but I didn't expect we'd actually find the things we did."[12]

NONCONSCIOUS PROBLEM SOLVING

How can we tap into these abilities without the use of the thinking cap or TMS? What if we could somehow access the nonconscious mind without the expense of losing our existing thoughts? Can you switch off part of your brain? As noted earlier, higher-level complex information fills our consciousness, while the savant-style information crunching that researchers suggest precedes it is relegated to the nonconscious back rooms of the brain. Can these back rooms be accessed naturally without the assistance of TMS? Can we use ourselves as a blank canvas for sense making and tap into the brain more effectively? Can leaders:

switch off their thinking?

alter mind frames?

understand how customers think?

experience differences in thought processes as they occur?

see the raw data of the world as it is, as it is actually represented in the nonconscious mind?

change the brain's operating system rather than rewiring it?

plunge in and out of the conscious mind at will?

enable the mind to perform more effectively?

switch off parts of the brain and turn on other parts at will?

use mental exercises to help learn how to suppress some areas of the brain?

tap into and develop any hidden potential by passing the executive centre of the brain and doing things we could normally not do?

change the way they view their world and see it the way it really is?

discover hidden talents?

switch competencies on and off?

There are ways to circumvent the normal conscious flow of the brain without needing to buy brain-scanning equipment for your office! Leaders are not stuck only with their words. Nonconscious behaviour is accessible to anyone. There are methods, techniques, and exercises that can enable leaders to learn how to suppress some areas of the brain, tap into and develop dormant potential, and uncover how customers, employees and leaders think. There is enormous capacity in a receptive mind that values visuals, stories, myths, and metaphors, among other things. However, as leaders we must first have to overcome the inattentional blindness, biases, perceptions, paradigm paralysis, and immune systems that suppress new ideas and preserve the status quo.

We are intrinsically blind. We see only what we know. Is it possible to extricate ourselves from this intrinsic blindness? Is it possible to see the world the way it really is? Peter M. Senge, Art Kleiner, Charlotte Roberts, George Roth, Rick Ross, Bryan Smith, authors of *The Dance of Change*, state, "We have complex, well-developed immune systems that preserve the status quo."[13] These immune systems exist in every organization. They can handicap efforts to capitalize on customer and employee feedback, and can cause leaders to ignore needs. We can become prisoners of our own past success – we keep trying to do the same things that worked in the past, even though the circumstances require something different.

We only see this world through our point of view, our blueprint, our paradigm, and our context. We only see this world through our preconceptions derived from our knowledge, expertise, and past experiences. Unlike savants, we frequently do not see and hear the world as it is. The Talmud provides this insight: "We don't see things the way they are. We see things the way we are." Leaders have difficulty seeing with fresh eyes, and can be blinded by their paradigms or mindsets.

3

CHAPTER THREE:
LEADERS, DROP YOUR MINDSETS
AND TAP THE NONCONSCIOUS

Figure 3-1: What do you see? A rabbit, a duck, or both?[1]

If we only know about ducks, then we will only see a duck when looking at this drawing. However, if we only know about rabbits, then we will only see a rabbit. Familiarity with both rabbits and ducks gives us the luxury of having two possible interpretations. We see what we expect to see based on our experiences, and what we see is based on our interpretation, our perception.[2] "Beauty is in the eye of the beholder." Or as comedian George Carlin once said, "Ever notice that the people who drive faster than you are maniacs, and that the ones who drive slower than you are morons?" Indeed, mindsets do dictate our reality.

In the above drawing, neither the object itself nor its image on our retinas is changing. This is only one of many examples that can be used to demonstrate the distinction between *sensation* (the direct sensory recording) and *perception* (what we take that recording to mean), or, "what is happening to me" (sensation) from "what is happening out there" (perception).[3] There are six ways to access experience distinguished by the six sense faculties (eye contact, ear contact, nose contact, tongue contact, body contact, and mind contact), and six kinds of feelings distinguished by the contact from where they came.

Our perceptions are mind contact while the other five are sensory contact. Our perceptions or interpretations are very personal and we mentally extrapolate something to match our expectation. We don't see what is in our environment. Rather, we define first and then we see, we define first and then we hear. We project our preconceptions onto each situation so the particular reading depends on our particular expertise, experiences, and blueprints. To be really effective in a complex and volatile environment, we must see and hear the world in a new light using our sensing capabilities. It sounds easy, but it is very challenging. For example, take the problems involved with eyewitness testimony in criminal or civil proceedings. Despite the witness's heartfelt belief in the veracity of their evidence, they can be wrong from time to time. Our senses appear to select some data and reject others.

MENTAL MODELS

Through early learning and habit we perceive certain impressions as significant, while others are as if they were never perceived at all. Infants form mental models about how the world works and, as they receive new information from their environment, they modify their theories to better explain to themselves what they are seeing, hearing, and feeling.[4] As adults, we retain many of the explanations our early childhood brain developed. We often trivialize evidence (including textbook learning) that refutes the original mental model. We fall into what is called *premature cognitive commitment* – that is, we think we know, indeed, sometimes are sure we know – what's going on when we really don't.[5] Anything we repeat regularly drops out of our conscious mind. Once embedded, these early theories are difficult to dislodge. For example, the senses can appear to fail even to register accustomed sounds that require no response, like the noise of a passing underground train or the barking of a dog. At a higher level of mental structuring, we decide to accept or reject a thought, because it is not of interest to our present concern or not relevant to our mental scheme. For example, when looking for a word in the dictionary, our eye will fall on other miscellaneous words, which we will notice at a glance but deem as not relevant. The main difficulty lies in the extent to which the mind is active or contributes subjectively to perception. This relates closely to the question of how much of perception is an involuntary act or a voluntary act.

Unable to direct our attention to everything within our environment, the discursive mind usually either follows habit in its selections or decides consciously and autonomously, in that we choose what to perceive, notice, and pay further attention to. An important factor in mental motivation is the influence of primary needs and secondary desires on the nature of perception between what the mind "receives" and what it "projects."[6]

We see in other people what is in ourselves. This psychological stratagem is particularly noticeable with regard to our vices. We try to escape from our faults by denying them; we see them only as aspects of other people – it is always other people that are the source of conflict. Projection is the great determiner of perception. Our inner world of mind, thoughts, and needs influences the dynamic of projection on two levels, the sensory and the psychological.[7]

On the sensory level, the world perceived by an individual is a mental phenomenon developed from the interaction between the senses and sense objects. When the vibrations of the external world strike the various senses, they produce the corresponding responses of sight, sound, taste, touch, and smell. The mind synthesizes these sensory experiences and produces a picture, which is then projected onto the external environment, creating the appearance of a world "out there." The apparently concrete external world is actually a mental image projected onto abstract patterns of sensory data. On the psychological level, an individual projects needs onto the sensory world, thereby creating their unique experience.

FILTERING CONSCIOUSNESS THROUGH PARADIGMS

Dexter Dunphy, distinguished professor at the University of Technology in Sydney, Australia states:

We live in the present with a map drawn in the past. Our mental models are worn hand-me-downs. These models and maps also carry with them built-in action programs that are past due. These structures form the very categories of our perceptions. So we are stuck in the residues of mind models that were once fresh and vibrant but are now irrelevant for understanding the new age bearing down upon us. So often we move forward in time like zombies, programmed by the past, our sensitivity deadened by the media, substituting slogans for thought, habit for experience, sullen conformity for innovation.[8]

Filtering consciousness through paradigms is like pushing play dough through a press with different designs at the end: whatever design we choose gives play dough its shape. So too with consciousness: whatever mindsets or paradigms we choose determine the form of our perceptions, which in turn shape our decisions, actions, experiences, social systems, worlds, and futures. Paradigms function like the software for human life. When the software does its job well, everything works and problems are solvable. But when the software is full of bugs or is not equal to the job, systems will freeze and fail, and nothing works as expected.

PARADIGMS: MINDSETS AND PATTERNS

The leader's brain uses paradigms to classify, sort, and process information received by the senses. Paradigms shape perceptions and practices in nearly nonconscious and unquestioned ways. Paradigms shape what we look at, how we look at things, what we label as challenges, what challenges we decide to address, and what methods we use. It is a way of filtering and making sense of all the information that bombards us everyday.[9] Ten years ago, paradigms were rarely applied to the analysis of organizations. Now, organizations regularly discuss and strategize about shifting paradigms. The idea that organizations can shift their paradigms is extremely powerful. It means that individuals and groups can redefine how they view and interpret the world around them, and begin to organize behaviour around new ways of thinking that can significantly transform organizations.

Paradigms are fundamental beliefs about the world. They provide needed rules and regulations, and establish boundaries and indicate behaviours that are needed to succeed. Paradigms also suggest metaphors that are helpful in framing problems which can lead to their ultimate solutions. However, paradigms can blind individuals to facts, data, and challenges that are not consistent with their thinking. The problem is that while we have the ability to think in new paradigms, our minds are optimized to think with existing paradigms. Our minds take in inputs from the world through the subprocesses of perception, and then retrieve patterns from memory (our past experiences) to make sense of these inputs. We don't even need the whole pattern or a perfect match; our minds are flexible enough to provide an explanation for the world in all its variety.

This flexible pattern-matching mechanism gives us many human abilities that we take for granted. For example, it enables a good troubleshooter to quickly zero in on a problem in a piece of equipment based on an initial review of the situation. The troubleshooter has seen the pattern of failure before and, therefore, has a good idea as to what caused the underlying breakdown. We call this natural mental ability *experience*. The mental mechanism is the same whether we are preparing a budget or just trying to get out of bed in the morning. We use the past experiences stored in our memory as a guide for how to proceed. An enormous amount of energy is needed to break apart an old paradigm. Ways of thinking are held onto both deeply and nonconsciously.

Our point of view, or sets of rules and regulations about what is going on in the world *allows for shortcuts in decision-making*. As a consequence, we are vulnerable to bias in the form of illusions and assumptions. Simply put, there is a cost for adopting any strategy that accelerates our decision-making process. Nothing can be seen within a neutral frame of reference. Anyone who doubts this fact should be reminded of the myriad of illusions, jokes, and puzzles that capitalize on our bias toward prior knowledge. For example, consider these two sentences:

The surgeon is waiting for the boy's father before sending him home. Coincidentally, the boy is the surgeon's son.

Now, these sentences will only appear puzzling if we have a blueprint that tells us all surgeons are male. Yet, everyone knows that there are female surgeons and male nurses. Even so, our minds still jump to the most familiar possibility instead of logically sifting through alternatives.

Only a savant brain sees the world unfiltered through prior knowledge. However, this comes at the enormous price of being unable to cope with decision-making. For example, savants and dementia patients observe the world without interpretation or expectation.[10] Everything for them must be evaluated anew. Basically, they lack paradigms, heuristics, or mindsets with which to conceptualize. They compensate for this loss with repetitive and stereotyped behaviour.

Clearly the use of pattern matching and paradigms are a masterful strategy which allows us to operate automatically in familiar situations. However, they come at the unavoidable cost of bias. We only see a filtered version of the world. What could possibly be the survival value of a strategy that is so susceptible to faults?

Powerful images distort our view and this may also create biases and perhaps even prejudices. A powerful new psychological tool, *The Implicit Association Test*, shows that as many as 90 to 95 percent of us display nonconscious roots of prejudice. The test developed by University of Washington psychology professor Anthony Greenwald and Yale professor Mahzarin Banaji (now at Harvard), measures people's implicit or nonconscious evaluations and beliefs about groups. It does so by testing the strong automatic associations people make – even people who regard themselves as nonprejudiced. Bias and prejudice are only a few of many assumptions we nonconsciously use when interpreting our visual world.[11]

BLUEPRINTS AND TEMPLATES

I want to emphasize that there is no definitive interpretation of the raw information that bombards our senses. It would take an eternity for our brains to work through all the possibilities. Besides, we have no interest in all the possibilities, only the most likely ones. So, we have evolved a rather cunning strategy for rapid decision-making. We make assumptions about what is most likely. Our brains do this by constructing blueprints about what is familiar and important. These blueprints act as templates through which we view the world. Our blueprints facilitate rapid decision-making.

Our points of view or perspectives allow for shortcuts in decision-making. They allow us to manoeuvre rapidly in familiar situations. But as a consequence of our blueprints, we are vulnerable to prejudice in the form of illusions.

While our flexible pattern-matching system of thinking is great for accomplishing the repetitive tasks of daily life and for coping with uniqueness in situations, it is not optimal when we want to respond to new information and create new ideas. Pattern matching and paradigms have a consequence. We pay a heavy price for our expertise, knowledge, and experience. We pay a heavy price for our nonconscious assumptions. That price is inattentional blindness: if you always do what you always did, you will always get what you always got.

YOU SEE MORE THAN YOUR EYE DOES

Through their experiments, Daniel Simons and Daniel Levin, two psychologists at Harvard University, have identified the phenomenon of *inattentional blindness*, which refers to the fact that individuals will not identify obvious changes in their environment if they do not pay attention overtly to the specific features exhibited in that environment.[12] Other scientists have agreed that individuals only record that which is relevant at the time. Evidently, attention is required to see change; without it, people will look at but not see the change. The eye doesn't see as much as we would like to think.

When our eyes are still, we detect changes easily, but when a change occurs during an eye movement or a blink, we are blind to that change. This fact illustrates both the strengths and weaknesses of visual attention. Leaders can effectively filter the visual world, devoting attention to some features while ignoring others. However, this process of selective attention can have costs as well, and these costs can be quite dramatic. People often fail to notice unexpected events, particularly when they are selectively attending to other aspects of their visual world.

SIGNAL DETECTION THEORY

How strong is a signal required to be before a leader can say that they have seen it? The answer depends not only on the strength of the signal, but also on the sensitivity of the leader (influenced by noise and focus of attention) and the criterion adopted by the leader (influenced by motivation or expectation).[13]

Noise is present both in the environment and in the sensory system of the leader. The leader reacts to the momentary total activation of the sensory system, which fluctuates from moment to moment. The leader also responds to environmental stimuli, which may include a signal. When leaders are asked whether they have detected a signal, they will respond affirmatively if their neural systems have reached a certain criterion level of intensity.

Because noise can sometimes look like a signal (or vice versa), the responses of the leader can fall into four categories: the probability that the leader will respond "yes" when a signal is present (a hit); the probability that the leader will respond "no" when a signal is present (a miss); the probability that the leader will respond "yes" when the target signal is not present (a false alarm); and the probability that the leader will respond "no" when the signal is not present (a correct rejection).[14]

THE SELECTIVE ATTENTION TASK

What are the implications of this experiment for leadership and management? If leaders do not pay attention (realize and react to environmental changes), their competencies, which are built upon certain beliefs and trends, can become rigidities. Further clarification of this tendency is provided by Gary Hamel, visiting professor of strategic and international management at the London Business School and chairman of Strategos, a business strategy firm. In his book, *Leading the Revolution*, Hamel says:

> corporate boundaries and orthodoxies - the deeply held beliefs of leaders about the scope and capabilities of their organization - act as blinders that prevent leaders from identifying opportunities outside the organization's traditional work. And whereas corporate boundaries are becoming increasingly permeable by means of virtual or Internet technology, free-agent workers, and open-source movements, such boundaries still often serve as relatively rigid business demarcation in the mind of leaders.[15]

Hamel also notes that many managers are both unable to see industry changes and unable to appreciate the impact of those changes on their industry. He states that "managers fail to anticipate or adequately respond to change for three reasons:

they simply fail to notice the changes and are unaware, they fail to interpret these changes correctly, and even if some managers notice the changes and they interpret them correctly, they might still fail to adopt an appropriate course of action. It is often competitors from outside an industry who change the face of competition within the industry – precisely because they are not constrained by conventional views."[16]

The reason for an organization's blindness, Hamel argues, "is an unwillingness or inability to look outside of current experiences," in other words, to look outside of mindsets. Helping organizations cure this type of blindness has been the latest focus of his work. Hamel says he aims to:

> systematically deconstruct the orthodoxies and dogmas that rule a business. When people think about strategy, frequently they take ninety or ninety five percent of industry paradigms as a given and as a constraint. Instead, they must stare down their orthodoxies (mindsets) and determine that they are not going to be bound by them anymore. In effect, in looking for new directions, they are simply not going to start with the same old starting point. They will start with a blank canvas.[17]

PARADIGM SHIFT

We don't often acknowledge the depth of inattentional leader blindness. We talk of "changing mindsets" as if it were a matter of pressing a button. The general idea is that we need a paradigm shift to move our mindset up into a new gear. All we have to do is think and look at our surroundings clearly for what is truly there, and the paradigm shift is more likely to occur. Leaders need to challenge the mindsets, paradigms and blueprints of their industry, organization, team, and self to *see with fresh eyes.*

The historian and philosopher of science, Thomas Kuhn, in his landmark book, *The Structure of Scientific Revolutions*, developed the term paradigm shift.[18] Kuhn does not describe a paradigm shift primarily as an intellectual shift, but rather, a social shift. Scientists build theories or paradigms, he argues, based on key features of the landscape of knowledge that they can identify around them. Once these key features become the substructure for a theory, they become dogmas. Sooner or later, new generations begin to notice features of the landscape that don't fit the theory. As more of these features are noticed, the discontinuities with the ruling paradigm prompt new observers to propose a new theory.

Interestingly, Kuhn notes that very often, key features of the old ideas disappear in the new paradigm. The vocabularies, the important features of the landscape, are completely different. Both the new and old observers are looking at the landscape and see completely different things. Kuhn notes that what is clearly evident to one party is not seen by the other party and because the main pillars of a paradigm form its substructure, parties can become dogmatic. New paradigms gain force through a process of natural selection. They work better than the old ones, and more people grow into them and prosper because they work better. Adherents to the old paradigms do not prosper; they multiply slower, diminish and wither away.

DROP THE OLD PARADIGMS
WHEN THEY DON'T FIT ANYMORE

Karl Weick, the author of *Drop Your Tools: An Allegory for Organizational Studies*, further clarifies these leadership attentional issues:

> In 1949, 13 firefighters lost their lives at Mann Gulch, and in 1994, 14 more firefighters lost their lives under similar conditions at South Canyon. In both cases, exploding fires overran these 23 men and four women. Their retreat was slowed because they failed to drop the heavy tools they were carrying. By keeping their tools, they lost valuable distance they could have covered more quickly if they had been lighter. All 27 perished within sight of safe areas.[19]

The question is why did the firefighters keep their tools? The imperative, "drop your tools or you will die," is the metaphor for leaders paradigms.

The reluctance to drop one's tools when threat intensifies is not just a problem for firefighters. Dropping one's tools is a leadership metaphor for unlearning, for engaging new perspectives and paradigms, for entertaining different ideas. It is the very unwillingness of people to drop their tools and paradigms that turns some of these dramas into tragedies.[20]

Abraham Kaplan was on target when he criticized what he called "law of instrument." Kaplan says, "Give a small boy a hammer, and he will find that everything he encounters needs pounding". The hammers of modern leadership are the traditional analytic tools used for problem solving and decision-making.[21]

The "law of the instrument" offers the pointed comment that leaders and managers often refuse to drop their paradigms, parables, and propositions even when their own personal survival is threatened. Their mindsets and the thousands of "scripts" that they act out when they are cued by something familiar blind them.[22]

FUNCTIONAL FIXEDNESS

Dunker in a classic problem solving experiment discovered that some subjects had difficulties solving certain puzzles due to a fixation on the purpose of one of the tools available to solve problems. During one experiment, which used a candle, a box of nails, and a hammer, subjects had to fix the candle to the wall so that it did not drip onto a table surface against the wall. Many attempts to nail or glue the candle to the wall were made by the subjects but few thought of using the box the nails came in as a candleholder and nailing it to the wall. The research noted that the subjects were fixated with the box's normal function (holding nails) and could not see its possible uses to them. Dunker termed this phenomena *functional fixedness*.[23]

Ellen Langer, a psychology professor at Harvard University, uses the term "mindlessness" to describe a leadership phenomenon similar to functional fixedness. She states that mindlessness is the application of yesterday's business tools to today's problems.[24] She goes on to say that "mindlessness is characterized by relying on past categories, acting on automatic pilot, precluding attention to new information and fixating on a single perspective. Trapped in previously created categories, these individuals easily confuse the stability of their assumptions with stability in the world, thus giving themselves a false reading on their surroundings."[25]

HOW DO WE KEEP UP?

Dropping one's tools as Weick advises, seeing with fresh eyes, being open to new paradigms and resisting mindlessness may be difficult in our complex environment. According to Thomas Davenport "we have built systems to bring information of every type to everyone and the consequence is that people are flooded with data, information, and knowledge, for which there is insufficient attention."[26] There is a battle for mindspace. According to Davenport, the average American white-collar worker sends and receives 220 messages per day in multiple media; there are over two billion Web pages on the Internet; the volume of Internet traffic doubles every one hundred days; voice mail, fax, and paper use are all up; 60% of office time is spent processing documents; and 76% of heavy Web users watch less television than before.[27]

PAY ATTENTION TO WHERE YOU PAY ATTENTION

Given the infoglut leaders find themselves in today, the relevant questions appear to be how does one *pay* attention, *hold* attention, and give attention to the right things? How can a leader's perception be improved to detect relevant changes in the environment? How can the diagnostic skills of leaders be improved with innovative concepts to diminish blindness to change and inattentional blindness? We need a new type of thinking that allows one to sense, tune into, and seize emerging opportunities. One way to clear the path to a new insight or idea is to shake up old routines and patterns of thinking; to hack away at a new trail through the jungle instead of taking the paved one, to see wonderful new things. Begin with a blank canvas; become more mindful and less mindless.

4

CHAPTER FOUR:
LEADING WITH MINDFULNESS:
TURNING OFF THE AUTOMATIC PILOT

We all think alike. No one thinks very much.
Walter Lippman

How can a leader cope with the uninvited guests of leadership?

- information overload;

- ambiguity and uncertainty;

- conflict between the needs of stakeholders;

- technical errors;

- contradictory evidence;

- unanticipated serious surprises/challenges;

- illusions of competence;

- lack of control.

The concepts of mindlessness and mindfulness have important implications for leaders. This chapter begins with examples of mindfulness and mindlessness in everyday life, and it proceeds to describe the negative effects of mindlessness in decision-making and how to overcome these effects with mindfulness.

MINDFULNESS

Paying attention to what you are doing while you are thinking about things (If you only have a hammer…).

According to Langer, the antidote to our old paradigms, mental models, blueprints and tools is mindfulness. Langer, who has researched and written about the topic for the last twenty-five years, states that we can break out of our debilitating mindsets by *leading with mindfulness*. Mindfulness is a counter to mental rigidity or mindlessness, which occurs when leaders lock themselves into ways of thinking. Mindfulness releases you from a dependence upon habitually referenced mindsets, and elevates your creative ability. As Langer states, mindfulness "leads the mind back from theories, attitudes and abstractions... to the situation of experience itself," which prevents us from "falling prey to our own prejudices, opinions, projections, expectations."[1]

According to Langer, mindfulness is a state of mind in which we are in the present, actively drawing distinctions, generating options, and asking questions.[2] Mindfulness is "a state of alertness and lively awareness that is manifested in active information processing, characterized by the creation and refinement of categories and distinctions and the awareness of multiple perspectives."[3] *Applying this concept to leadership, it can be argued that leaders must be mindful to constantly expand their categories. Leaders need to be interested in new ideas and concepts in their environments.*

A leader must also be open to different perspectives. A leader's willingness to listen and learn from others experiences speaks to a capability for growth. A leader, often faced with different perspectives, must be able to listen, learn, and in many cases, make effective decisions that navigate these views. Leaders who choose not to adopt new concepts or accept new ideas also fail to inspire employees or develop strong relationships and thereby make it challenging to communicate a vision or effect change. "In a world where ideas, intellectual capital, and an inspired and talented workforce are key competitive differentiators, a company whose leader is unwilling to listen to new ideas is prone to becoming a cataclysmic disaster."[4]

What is a mindful leader? They:

- have the flexibility to constantly create new categories,

- are open to new information, and open to novelty in general;

- actively notice new things and trends;

- keep situated in the present;

- maintain awareness of multiple perspectives on any idea or issue; are alert to distinctions;

- remain receptive to changes in contexts;

- retain orientation to the present;

- attend to process (doing) rather than only outcome (results);

- reframe information in an endless number of ways;

- think of rules as rough guides and not rigid formulas

- trust intuition;

- are involved in and enjoy what is being done.[5]

Mindlessness, on the other hand is characterized by:

- an entrapment in old categories;

- automatic behaviour that precludes attending to new signals;

- action that operates from a single perspective.[6]

Langer states, "Many problems are not solved because leaders think about them in automatic and habitual ways. This automatic mode of thought, called mindlessness, plays a role in how we think."[7] The cost of mindless thinking is significant because it leads to inattentional blindness and limits the leader's ability to make good decisions, recognize changes in other people, and see things from a variety of perspectives. When we perceive and react to our world in these inflexible ways, we stop ourselves from seeing other possibilities of action. The following excerpts from Langer's book, *Mindfulness*, illustrates the potential hazards of mindlessness: "When we are behaving mindlessly, that is to say, relying on categories drawn in the past, endpoints to development seem fixed. We are then like projectiles moving along a predetermined course. When we are mindful, we see all sorts of choices and generate new endpoints. Mindful involvement in each episode of development makes us freer to map our own course."[8]

Mindlessness occurs when we "blindly follow routines or unwittingly carry out senseless orders... we are acting like automatons, with potential grave consequences for ourselves and others."[9] The results of mindfulness, on the other hand, are more effective behaviour, more creative thinking, and an ability to move comfortably from one context to another.

CONSCIOUS PROCESSING

Mindlessness results when we don't know that the categories we subscribe to are in fact categories, having accepted them as our own without really thinking and tapping the nonconscious. In the last decade Langer developed the Langer's Mindfulness Scale (LMS) a twenty-one item questionnaire that assesses four domains associated with mindful thinking: novelty seeking, engagement, novelty producing, and flexibility. According to Langer, an individual who seeks novelty perceives each situation as an opportunity to learn something new. An individual who scores high in engagement is likely to notice more details about his or her specific relationship with the environment. A novelty - producing person generates new information in order to learn more about the current situation. Flexible people welcome a changing environment rather than resist it. Mindfulness or being mindful is being aware of your present moment. The mindful leader does not judge, reflect or think. The mindful leader simply observes the moment in which they find themselves.[10]

TRY THIS:

In your office, get quiet. Close your laptop or desktop, place your calls on hold, it's time for fifteen minutes of silence. Pay attention and notice what you notice during this time.

Doing this will remind you that leadership involves mindfulness: the art of paying attention and seeing things in a fresh way.

LANGUAGE OF MINDLESSNESS

Words such as "clearly" and "obviously" raise red flags for Langer. She says "Whenever I hear those words, I know there's mindlessness lurking there, because things are too complicated to be so clear and obvious."[11] She adds, "When you're mindless, your behaviour is rule- or routine-governed. It's the human tendency to operate on autopilot, whether by stereotyping; performing mechanically, by rote; or simply not paying attention. When you're mindful, your behaviour... is guided by these rules and routines, rather than being determined by them."[12] To be mindful means to choose differently. It challenges leaders to create new categories of understanding, to open themselves to new information, and to become aware of multiple perspectives and possibilities.

WHY MINDFULNESS?

Mindfulness cultivates the investigation of reality and challenges leaders about what they really know. If a leader already knows, the leader cannot be mindful. Their notions of conceptual reality imprison leaders, because knowing creates security, and we'd rather be secure than have direct experience of not knowing.

Mindfulness makes room for new ways of knowing, different ways of knowing, and the unknown. Mindfulness takes us beyond the limitations of cognition and the analytical mind.

THE MINDFUL LEADER'S BEHAVIOURS AND RESULTING BENEFITS

The mindful leader's behaviour can be described as:

- encouraging, more flexible, less stereotyped thinking about a range of situations;
- being the opposite of multitasking;
- exploiting the power of uncertainty so that they can learn what things can become novel distinction-drawing;
- learning that maintains an awareness of context and of the ever-changing nature of information;
- being aware of one's own mental processes;
- listening attentively;
- suspending judgment while pausing to observe facts:
- becoming flexible;
- recognizing bias and judgments;
- using nonjudgmental attention to self and others;
- attending to the ordinary, the obvious, and the present;
- engaging in moment-to-moment self-monitoring and reflective practice;
- bringing to consciousness their tacit personal knowledge and deeply held values;

- deferring action and applying the brakes to stop rash interference;

- slowing down thought, speech, and action;

- keeping still, stopping, pausing, and slowing down;

- using peripheral vision and subsidiary awareness;

- adopting curiosity in both ordinary and novel situations;

- interpreting all data, regardless of its completeness or accuracy to make sense of it and apply it to organizational life;

- being present in everyday experience, in all of its manifestations, including actions, thoughts, sensations, images, interpretations, and emotions.[13]

The benefits of mindful behaviour include:

- reductions in surprises because the leader better anticipates them coming and make smaller changes ahead of time;

- shifts in perspective problems are more likely to be viewed as opportunities rather than as failures. Being aware that failure is not a rigid category, but rather that it depends on the situation, helps leaders to move on to find success;

- being able to face any situation with a fresh mind, with clarity of vision unprejudiced by those first spontaneous responses;

- achieving clarity of vision, a direct view of reality, without any colored or distorted lenses, without the intrusion of emotional or habitual prejudices and intellectual biases or mindsets;

- comes face to face with the bare facts of actuality, seeing them as vividly and freshly as if we were seeing them for the first time;

- perceiving changes, re-direction and renewal in an ongoing situations;

- listening attentively to team members' voices, recognizing their own errors, refining their technical skills, making fact-based decisions, and clarifying their values;

- becoming aware of new information and perspectives.[14]

In contrast mindlessness results in:

- errors in judgment and technique;

- inattentional blindness;

- hardening of the categories;

- deviations from professionalism in emotionally charged situations, during situations of uncertainty, and under pressure to resolve problems;

- not being able to see small changes, those providing clues of things to come;

- reporting of findings that were not observed and do not seek correction for errors;

- actions that diverge from professional knowledge and values because of attempts to be efficient, a desire to please direct reports, feelings of embarrassment, and a sense of being overwhelmed;

- deviations often involving avoidance of difficult issues, rationalization, externalization, or frank denial rather than the healthy processing of emotional feelings toward team members/colleagues/ stakeholders or clients;

- learning without context awareness, which has severely limited uses and often sets one up for failure.

- trying to reduce uncertainty. As leaders we think we know things and thereby confuse the stability of our mindsets with the stability of the underlying phenomenon.[15]

Often the "autopilotness" of one's approach is not detected until some transforming experience occurs that inspires more complete engagement.

TRY THIS:

- Turn off the automatic pilot response in meetings;

- pay attention in a non-judgmental way, to what is going on in the mind, and in the environment;

- rather than focusing on gathering information focus on staying aware and be fully "present" in the here and now;

- employ "informed intuition" in decision-making;

- monitor thoughts and feelings;

- do not engage in unmindful consumption of data, and information;

- be imaginative and flexible in thinking.

HOW DOES MINDFUL THINKING WORK?

Remember that the process of consciousness (awareness) starts with the nonconscious brain. The nonconscious brain senses all reality before labelling it, and the conscious mind uses words to describe reality. Mindfulness is the reality which gives rise to words – it is nonconscious thinking, the words that follow are simply shadows of reality.

When one first becomes aware of something there is a fleeting instant of pure awareness just before one conceptualizes or identifies it. That is a stage of mindfulness. Ordinarily, this stage is very short. It is that flashing split second just before one focuses one's eyes on the thing, just before one focuses the mind on the thing, just before one objectifies it, clamps down on it mentally and segregates it from the rest of existence. This split second takes place just before one starts thinking about it, and identifying what it is. It is termed *precognition*, (before thinking).

Mindfulness is very much like what you see with your peripheral vision as opposed to the hard focus of normal or central vision. How can leaders prolong that moment of mindfulness and access the nonconscious for longer periods of time? Mindfulness sees, feels, tastes, and hears things as they really are. It adds nothing to perception and it subtracts nothing. It distorts nothing. It is bare attention and just looks at whatever comes up. Conscious thought on the other hand verbalizes our experience, provides us with concepts and ideas, and immerses us in plans. When mindful, you see something different. You notice exactly what arises in your mind, and then you notice the next thing to arise after that.

To be mindful, avoid what Langer calls the *premature cognitive commitment*, or making an initial impression without the benefit of critical thinking.[16] Develop a "beginner's mind" – the ability to always see things as new and open. Young children don't have to be taught mindfulness; they're naturally that way, ever in-the-moment and able to amuse themselves by playing with among other things, cardboard boxes.

How can organizations attain mindfulness? By having a healthier respect for uncertainty. When leaders are uncertain, they remain tuned in. If there's no uncertainty, mindlessness is the reality. Being mindful is a very simple process: it's simply noticing new things, seeing things differently than you did a moment ago, and differently from the way others might be directing you to see them. Being mindful keeps a leader engaged.

TRY THIS:

Practise the Habits of Mindful Practitioners

Beginner's Mind:
see with fresh eyes;
be willing to set aside categories and examine bias.

Presence:
diminish reactivity and control anxiety;
let go and avoid single-mindedness;
tolerate contradictory ideas;
get personally invested.

Attentive Observation:
observe the observer;
develop peripheral vision;
notice what you notice.

Critical Curiosity:
ask reflective and open-ended questions;
tolerate (and enjoy) being wrong.

Being mindful and attaining more of the practices mentioned earlier can be a function of trying the following:

- be open and willing to involve yourself in new experiences (concrete experience);

- develop your observational and reflective skills so that these new experiences can be viewed from a variety of perspectives (reflective observation);

- develop analytic, creative and empathic abilities so integrative ideas and concepts can be created from observation (abstract conceptualization);

- develop decision-making and problem solving skills so these new ideas and concepts can be used in actual practice (active experimentation);

- develop metacognitive skills (mindfulness) so that you can reflect upon and learn about your approach to thinking, learning, and acting as a basis for continual improvement in your efficacy (intellectual self -management).

Mindfulness can be inspired by actively drawing distinctions.[17] Noticing new things about the target, no matter how small or trivial the distinctions may be, reveals that it looks different from different perspectives. For example, when we learn our facts in a conditional way, we are more likely to draw novel distinctions and thus stay attentive to context and perspective.

HOW OFTEN ARE WE MINDLESS?

Langer says "much of the time we are mindless. Of course we are unaware when we are in that state of mind because we are 'not there' to notice. To notice, we would have had to be mindful. Yet over twenty-five years of research reveals that mindlessness may be very costly to us."[18]

There are a number of common cognitive errors leading to mindlessness and inattentional blindness:

- irrational aversion to regret;

- cognitive dissonance: a belief clearly contradicted by evidence, usually longheld;

- anchoring: a tendency to be inappropriately influenced by external suggestions;

- status quo bias: a tendency to take bigger gambles;

- compartmentalization: a tendency to limit choices by premature assignment to a category often with little basis;

- overconfidence in one's answers;

- representativeness heuristic: treating events as representative of some well-known class in the absence of sufficient data; a tendency to see patterns where none exist;

- availability heuristic: focusing excessive attention on details that are close at hand rather than on the big picture;

- magical thinking: attributing to one's own actions something that has nothing to do with them;

- quasi-magical thinking: behaving as if one believes ones thoughts can influence events even when one knows they can't;

- hindsight bias: once something happens, a tendency to overestimate the ability to predict it in the future;

- memory bias: a tendency to falsely think you have predicted things that happened;

- emotional bias: cutting off the nose to spite the face.[19]

THE BEGINNER'S MIND

Leaders need to develop a "beginner's mind" – the ability to see things as new and open. Much of what we do in organizations is based on the idea of finding the right answer to a question. Unfortunately it is often assumed there is only right answer, we do not need to think about the topic further. In real life, much of what is known is in a state of flux, waiting for a new bit of evidence to modify the knowledge. Recent discoveries in science, for example, have greatly modified our understanding of the brain and how it works. What is true in science is also true in almost every aspect of life. We have fostered a one-right-answer mentality in a conditional world.

Mindfulness is a discipline and an attitude of mind. It requires critical informed curiosity and courage to see the world as it is rather than how one would have it be. Mindful leaders tolerate making conscious their previously nonconscious actions and errors. The goal of mindfulness is to use a wide array of data and categories in order to make informed choices and decisions, thereby avoiding inattentional blindness.

5

CHAPTER FIVE:
FRESH PERCEPTION: ART AND LEADERSHIP,
IS THERE A SYNERGY?

Our perceptive capacities may be more important than we had ever imagined.[1]
Ellen Langer

MAKING UNEXPECTED CONNECTIONS

Ultimately, the driving force for new leadership is the process of *destroying one's own mindset to build a completely new picture*. As Sigmund Freud said: "I am not really a man of science, I am not an observer, I am not an experimenter, I am not even a thinker. I am nothing but an adventurer - a conquistador - with all the boldness, and the tenacity of that type of being."[2] In other words, from his own assessment, Freud was not especially skilled or talented. Rather, he had the courage to break the rules and to confront conventional wisdom, to access alternate paradigms.

Research by Cap Gemini Ernst & Young's Center for Business Innovation located in Cambridge Massachusetts, suggests the most reliable source of new ideas is the recombination of existing thinking through the interaction of people with diverse knowledge, disciplines, experiences, and values.[3] Breakthrough ideas that turn into an innovation are rare. More often, existing ideas are brought together in a new way or in a new context that opens up new possibilities. This sort of recombination can only happen if heterogeneous and diverse people are given the opportunity to interact with each other.

Increasing connectivity creates opportunities for recombination. According to the Center for Business Innovation, "connecting like-to-like may give you mass, but it won't give you innovation."[4] Innovation is largely about making unexpected connections between diverse things by flexing all of our brain, and pursuing ideas from multiple sources.

Is it difficult to question the value of bringing divergent concepts and findings together? Who would object to translating, integrating, and synthesizing competing claims, data, and conclusions; borrowing useful information and techniques from cooperating disciplines; revealing unexpected similarities and parallels; and, finally, interrelating diverse, competing, and isolated fields? As Zaltman says, "I don't buy the notion that the world is organized the way universities and companies are. Ideas don't know what discipline they're in. We might kidnap them and say, 'That's a management idea' or 'That's an anthropology idea.' But if you walked up to an idea on the street, it wouldn't know about that."[5]

The relation between the sciences and the humanities has been marked more by opposition than by cooperation. The sciences, proudly insist on objectivity, quantification, and control. The humanities just as strongly promote the virtues of subjectivity, intuition, and narration. The commonalities that underlie both disciplines – a reliance on rational rules of discovery, sensitivity to irresolvable intricacies, and a search for truth – are submerged and forgotten.

The sciences and the humanities, business and art face each other with conflicting and incompatible profiles, so that relatively narrow facts disclosed by the sciences are not related to the larger contexts discussed by the humanities, and the insights used through visualization are not related to the logical analysis of decision-making. Wolfgang Ernst Pauli, a Nobel Prize laureate in physics, insisted that in the future one could no longer ignore the relationships between knowledge of the external material world and the inner world of meaning-giving contents of the human mind.[6] Leaders have to acknowledge the rational scientific approach as but one way of seeing and interpreting the world. How can leaders open the windows of nonconsciousness? How can a leader see the world with mindfulness?

Today, leadership practices focus primarily on what is visible.[7] However, this provides real challenges in today's knowledge-based global economy, where things are not always what they appear to be. Leaders and managers increasingly face complex environments, and deal with ambiguous information and unanalyzable tasks. Even with such incomplete knowledge and inferior plans, they must take action anyway.

UNFAMILIAR AND VOLATILE ENVIRONMENTS

Leaders continually find themselves at the edge of their competencies. How can they respond effectively? How do you identify ways to help people handle unfamiliar situations, and how do you identify ways to help people know they are in unfamiliar situations? Albert Einstein once said, "we can't solve problems by using the same kind of thinking we used when we created them."

If leaders are dealing with the familiar (habitual, everyday, well-structured, clear) *routine thinking suffices*. However, when dealing with the novel (fluid, new, unfamiliar, ill-structured, chaotic) *nonroutine thinking is required.*[8] We need to map the invisible territory of leadership and develop a deeper level of awareness by tapping the nonconscious; seeing and hearing with fresh eyes and ears.

Successful leaders recognize that there are many ways of framing reality and will consequently use the necessary tools. First-rate leaders go to the root. They don't just ask what's appropriate or what framework can be dug up and imposed. They will study the situation from many angles much like a photographer or artist would, to fundamentally determine what is really going on. They may borrow ideas and cobble together a very different framework. Obviously, taking on additional mindsets, frames of reference, paradigms, framework, and models in short to become more mindful is useful - the more mindsets leaders can imbue, the more different angles and snapshots can be created.[9]

AESTHETICS AND THE ARTS

The term "aesthetic" derives from the Greek word for perception - *aistheta*.[10] The ability to see and hear what's coming, and to make sense of it is usually associated with artists, not business leaders. For example, there are three ways to look at a painter and the painter's work: one can look at the completed painting; one can watch the artist in the process of painting; or one can watch the painter before the brush is lifted, as they consider the blank canvas.[11] Each structural perspective offers a different type of access to the artist's work.

The completed picture is the explicit reflection of the artist's work. The artist, in the process of painting, offers insight into the skills and knowledge brought to the work. The artist in front of the blank canvas senses the emergent painting, much as Michelangelo, in talking about his famous sculpture of David, sensed the emergent figure: "David was already in the stone. I just took away everything that wasn't David." The ability to **see** a David where others just see rock is what distinguishes the truly great artist. The same applies to leaders.[12] As J. Jaworski, founder of the American Leadership Forum (ALF), says: "The capacity to

Figure 5-1: Tools of the painter.

see what is there, make sense of it and seize the opportunities distinguishes great entrepreneurial leaders from the rest."[13] Today, leaders increasingly find themselves standing in front of their own blank canvases. They are faced not only with the challenge of figuring out what in their environment may contain the potential new "David" but also with, how to take away everything that *isn't* David. In order to learn how to intuit emergent form, leaders have to access a new type of not-yet-embodied knowledge."[14] Or as Johann Sebastian Bach is reported to have said, when asked how he found melodies: "The problem is not finding them, it's when getting up in the morning and out of bed not stepping on them."

As is supported by brain research, capacities used in the fine arts provide intriguing possibilities to improve a leader's sense, perception, and interpretation skills.

WHAT LEADERS CAN LEARN FROM PAINTERS

Imagine yourself as a painter. How do you bring the painting into being? *It begins in the mind's eye.* Looking and seeing are not the same thing. Those of us who are untrained often look, but do not see what we are looking at. In contrast, painters go through extensive training to see what there is to see, to see with innocent eyes. They must be fluent in the reality they are observing, and fluent in the way they represent it on paper or canvas.

There is only one way to see more than you are seeing, and that is to look at reality from a different vantage point. Semir Seki a professor of Neurobiology at University College London, notes painters have understood something about the visual brain.[15] Seki claims that artists are like neurologists, studying the brain with techniques that are unique to them and reaching interesting but unspecified conclusions about the organization of the brain.[16] Artists through trial and error have learned the same methods or more scientifically, the same algorithms evolved by our nonconscious brain for extracting the quintessential attributes of the natural visual world. They have temporarily released their artistic capability by preventing interference from higher-level conscious thinking. Many painters constantly strive to look with an innocent or beginner's eye. Artists see what they are able to paint, but they can't paint what they already see.

A painter does not paint with the eye but paints with the brain.[17] What is the neurological basis of the uniquely aesthetic experiences associated with art? The brain controls everything we see, hear, feel, and do. Leaders don't see what is actually out there; they actively seek and extract information about the environment. And, this is the fundamental block to seeing clearly.

The brain of a leader possesses the necessary visual information required to draw; yet few of us are able to access it for the purpose of drawing. However, if we could be conscious of how we see, we would find that our brain employs the same strategies as artists.[18] Our brain is not a passive photographer of the visual world, it is a processor of data. So how does a leader invite their brain to encounter thoughts that might not otherwise be encountered? It is possible to explore the intersection of the different domains of art and leadership by using our conscious and nonconscious brains and improving our practices as developing leaders.

IS ARTFUL LEADERSHIP THE ANSWER?

Walk through the public area of many of today's large corporations and you'll find the walls and atria lined with artworks. Paintings and sculpture are as much a part of the trappings of corporate success as the corporate private jet. Traditionally, art and commerce are separated and not considered bedfellows. When David Kelly founder of IDEO (arguably the world's most influential design firm), wrote the *Art of Innovation* the result was raised eyebrows in both the artistic and corporate communities.[19] Business leaders see themselves as practical problem solvers. Use the word "creative" and it had best be followed by "solution." In business, "creativity" and "art" are most frequently confined to marketing and advertising departments.

In his classic work, *What is Art?*, the Russian writer Leo Tolstoy argues that the point of art is not the product, but the process.[20] The processes of art are comprised of sensing, curiosity, visualization, perception, engagement, absorption, sonicity, improvisation, and movement, among other things. Metaphors, visualization, imagery, and enhanced perception are the key ways of thinking and knowing in the world of art. Art can incorporate literature, music, drama, visual arts and dance, or a combination thereof. It is through art that we can look at the world with different lenses and look for emerging themes.

By working in partnership with artists or using artistic processes, leaders can explore new approaches to issues and experience new ways of thinking. For many leaders, this will be an entirely new approach, but one that may be worth exploring. In fact art may become leadership's new paradigm. The arts represent different ways of seeing and experiencing the reality of the world, of strengthening various intelligences, and the arts are a practical way to access the power of the aesthetic.

In our complex world, our perceptive capacities may be more important than we had ever imagined. A leading business management writer, Peter Drucker, argues that we are in the midst of evolutionary transformation from analysis as the organizing principle of life, to one where perception is at the centre. Information based societies are organized around meaning, and meaning requires at its heart common perception. He says:

> In governmental and business planning we increasingly talk of 'scenarios' in which perception is the starting point. And, of course ecology is perception rather than analysis. In an ecology, the 'whole' has to be seen and understood, and the 'parts' exist only in contemplation of the whole.[21]

Drucker observes that by teaching the arts as the rigorous disciplines they are, we could enhance our perceptive capacities.

Steve Zades, chairman and CEO of Long Haymes Carr (LHC), an advertising agency based in Winston-Salem, North

Carolina, asserts that in today's world, "contemporary art is the R&D lab of the future."[22] Zades, whose credentials include a masters degree in business from Columbia University and experience working at Procter & Gamble, grew up playing guitar and the cello. Zades feels it may be time to shatter some dichotomies and polarities: "I see the intersection of business and art as the new frontier."[23] That's why Zades exposes both his employees and his clients to what's new at museums, in the theatre and on the street. His rationale is that this enables one to make connections and linkages in new and diverse places; to gain fresh perspectives; to look outside and create new combinations of images.[24]

We rely primarily on analysis and reason and seek little understanding from our sensations, perceptions, intuitions, insights, feelings, and emotions. Yet there is power in balancing reason with perception.

In his book *Art as Experience*, John Dewey writes of the unique ability of the arts.[25] By setting leaders on a lifelong journey with the arts, we encourage ongoing informed perception, appreciation and relationship with the people of the world, to "break through the crust of conventionalized and routine consciousness."[26] Dewey felt that artists, "have always been the real purveyors of news, for it is not the outward happening in itself which is new, but the kindling by it of emotion, perception and appreciation."[27] When we begin to create and respond to the arts ourselves, we inspire perception and appreciation. We look underneath the surface realities of the world. We release our imagination.

The way our senses engage and are engaged by the world is too often taken as a natural phenomenon divorced from the social relations of everyday life. Because of the connection between our senses and the outside world, when we talk about perception and decision-making we are also talking about how we think. What simple methods can leaders use to increase the quality and quantity of aesthetic experiences in their lives? Do artists have a sixth sense that allows them to perceive the world better? No. They just know what to look for, and leaders can learn how to look for it as well.[28]

Joseph Jaworski and Claus Otto Scharmer in *Sensing and Actualizing Emerging Futures*, focus on perception and alternate ways of thinking to describe what they perceive to be essential practices for leadership. They have identified five core practices for leaders.[29]

The first practice is observation of environments and full engagement with the contexts at issue, which allows one to see reality with fresh eyes. The viewing and interpretation of works of art, and engagement with art provides visual training and enforce accurate observation in order to make meaning. The results lead to nonconscious application of improved visual capabilities on daily life in general and, more specifically, regarding the organizational environment.

Jaworski and Scharmer's second practice is sensing. It refers to turning the perceived into "emerging patterns that inform future possibilities."[30] A multi-perspective on issues directly allows better decision-making, because more details are considered and the problem of oversimplification can be reduced.

The third and fourth practices are presencing and envisioning. Presencing describes the accessing of the leader's inner source of creativity and will. The willingness to use and augment the personal creativity reservoir and open-mindedness toward unusual concepts increases the ability to think, out of the box. Envisioning reflects the capability to develop a clear vision and implement it into the organization. The application of newly acquired skills affects the performance of management and in consequently the performance of the organization as a whole.

Jaworski and Scharmer's last practice is enacting. Enacting means the translation of improved managerial perception into measurable action, either on an individual or organizational basis. This may involve individual decisions about product development or general strategies. The actions taken are indispensable preconditions to assess effects of changed behaviour. Reflection and imagination stand for different levels of cognition. On the reflective level, humans modify and adapt their mental models, while on the level of imagination they broaden their focus away from objects more to the related source.

In *The Leader's Edge: Six Creative Competencies for Navigating Complex Challenges*, Chuck Palus and David Horth make the case that most leaders do not use all of the competencies at their disposal.[31] They set out additional neglected ways of leading, what they call creative leadership competencies – paying attention, personalizing, imaging, serious play, co-inquiry, and crafting – and show what they mean and how to use them to increase effectiveness when confronting turbulence. Palus and Horth invoke leaders to learn to look at their challenges through new eyes and construct fresh solutions by applying these six creative competencies: "These 'meaning-making' competencies can be learned through visual arts, dialogue and shared inquiry, innovative problem solving tools, poetry and music."[32]

LEONARDO da VINCI

Historically, Leonardo da Vinci (1452-1519) embodied the coming together of arts and science. Tony Buzan and Raymond Keene in Buzan's *Book of Genius and How to Unleash Your Own* rank Leonardo da Vinci as the greatest genius.[33] A remarkable Renaissance man, da Vinci was a terrific role model for applying the conscious and nonconscious brain innovatively in every aspect of life including art and music. Although he is best known for his dramatic and expressive artwork, da Vinci also conducted dozens of carefully thought out experiments and created futuristic inventions before modern science and invention had really begun.

da Vinci saw how machines could save people time and effort, and he used his creativity and his understanding of machinery to design and sketch his inventions. He built prototypes and created finished blueprints for his inventions. He produced studies on varied subjects, including nature, flying machines, geometry, mechanics, municipal construction, canals, and architecture (designing everything from churches to fortresses).[34] His studies from this period contain designs for advanced weapons, including a tank and other war vehicles, various combat devices, and submarines. Also during this period, he produced his first anatomical studies.

Michael J. Gelb, recognized as a pioneer in the fields of creative thinking, accelerated learning, and innovative leadership, articulated da Vinci's principles in his book *How to Think Like Leonardo da Vinci: Seven Steps to Genius Every Day.*[35]

The seven principles are:

Curiosita: an insatiably curious approach to life and an unrelenting quest for continuous learning.

Dimostarzione: a commitment to test knowledge through experience, persistence, and a willingness to learn from mistakes.

Sensazione: the continual refinement of the senses, especially sight, as the means to enliven experience.

Sfumato: a willingness to embrace ambiguity, paradox, and uncertainty.

Arte/Sciena: the development of the balance between science and art, logic and imagination. "Whole brain" thinking.

Corporalita: the cultivation of grace, ambidexterity, fitness, and poise.

Connessione: a recognition and appreciation for the interconnectedness of all things and phenomena, systems thinking.

These principles, along with the other research that has been presented clearly invoke the connections between disciplines and the use of conscious and nonconscious processes. These principles will be integrated in the following chapters, and tools will be described to assist leaders in dealing with complexity.

6

CHAPTER SIX:
DEVELOPING THE LEADER'S
DISCOVERY CAPACITY

I dream for a living.
Steven Spielberg

SEE what everyone else has seen,
THINK what no one else has thought, and
DO what no one else has dared.
Author unknown

In this chapter we begin to explore the leadership process and core practices required to tap the nonconscious brain and lead in an era of complexity. In the following chapter we learn specific leadership tools to access the nonconscious brain.

We need different ideas and fresh approaches to make sense of what's happening in the world. Leaders would be well served to pull out a blank canvas and act more like an artist rather than constrict themselves to a fixed rulebook dominated by analysis. Metaphors and the world of art can assist leaders by providing the process and tools to use multiple modes of perception to understand complexity and overcome the built-in bias that many organizations exhibit. Opening the windows of consciousness, transporting what may exist below a leader's level of awareness can be a complex and revealing process, but the results are often fascinating.

THE BLUEPRINT AND THE BLANK CANVAS

For our purposes we will use the blueprint metaphor to describe the conventional leadership paradigm. Current leadership thinking utilizes many blueprints to develop and enact strategies, metrics, processes, information technology, deliverables, and people. Many leadership practices use words not images, relying primarily on e-mails, meetings, communiqués, PowerPoint, spreadsheets, and Blackberry's. Yet sociolinguists know that much of communication is nonverbal. However most tools to access and discover people's thoughts and strategies are verbal or word based.

The blueprint may inhibit seeing and hearing what's out there: blueprints protect us from danger, but can also inhibit our capacity to respond to dramatically new situations that are uncertain, hard to achieve consensus on and complex. Leaders also need to engage perception and the nonconscious through images and voices to give meaning to facts and to facilitate innovative or transformational thinking. Blueprints have survival value, and can also be a liability in a rapidly changing world in which old categories no longer seem to apply. Blueprints allow leaders to make judgments, evaluate, trust the known, identify consequences, label phenomena, seek closure, structure situations, create rules, detect threats, engage caution through risk management, and avoid surprises.

Just as the old leadership paradigm is expressed as a metaphor of the blueprint, the new leadership paradigm can be expressed as a metaphor as well. It is known as the blank canvas.

HOW ARE YOU PAINTING YOUR CANVAS?

With every experience, you alone are painting your own canvas, thought by thought, choice by choice.
Oprah Winfrey

All leaders have a "canvas" that they are working with. The canvas has been painted and is full of ideas, paradigms, models, beliefs, behaviours, values, and habits. Furthermore, every canvas in their organizations has also already been painted. Leaders create their own canvas, their own reality and world view. They interact with all of their surroundings, using their conscious (aware) mind to draw on tools and experiences to create their canvas. As a leader, are you aware of what is on your canvas?

Figure 6-1: Paintings on Rue St. Germain in Paris

THE PAINTED CANVAS

What if leaders could become aware of their nonconscious thinking, their painted canvas, and see their blindspots, see their mindsets, see what motivates them, and see the world as it really is? What if leaders could assess their past performance as if it were a completed piece of art? Some areas of this canvas might seem a bit scattered; perhaps the wrong brush was used. Other areas may seem too dark, perhaps the leader was discouraged by the economy. The middle of the canvas might be overwhelmingly bright and full of colour, this could be where the leader got it right.

Leaders need to be open-minded when interpreting their canvas. Everyone is free to interpret art differently, no matter what the artist's intention. What if leaders permitted themselves the opportunity to change what needed to be changed, to begin with a blank canvas. If what was needed was to switch the old brush for a new one, to change from bolds to pastels, or if what was needed was a much larger canvas for the coming year, all of this could be done.

Leaders can ask for a blank slate, or in Latin, a tabula rasa, so that the nonconscious mind can inscribe entirely new, entirely fresh chapters onto their organizational life. There is power in the invitation of the blank canvas, clearing the mind, or getting rid of preconceptions, letting go of outmoded paradigms. However, leaders are often afraid of being without their mindsets. They hold onto their mindsets, strategies, financial plans, and people. They would simply like to turn the page. The blank canvas challenges this. It says, "It is all right to not have every role occupied. It is all right to be without." The blank canvas opens up new options.

Whatever the profession, the starting point for the entire leadership process is the blank slate, a clean canvas on which we can paint a landscape. Leaders can be artists, standing before a blank canvas, and can have the singularly unique and rewarding ability to reinvent themselves and their organizations. The leader's ideas, visions, and dreams are the colours used to create the painting. Together, leaders can take the brush, use a set of paints, and begin to paint a new picture, guiding the team of artists in the organization, where everyone paints different ideas on the canvas.

The blank canvas is part of the receiving mind, which is also void of judgment. It is the willingness not to fill up all the space in our lives, the willingness to let go of images. Leaders let themselves become empty, so that they may be written on. It may look like nothing is there, but the truth is that nothing is missing. If leaders are able to wake up and become more aware of what moves and motivates them, they will see that they have picked up the paintbrush; they are painting the shapes of their thoughts and feelings on that blank canvas. The leader is the artist and therefore anything can be painted. What the leader paints is as ephemeral as anything else in life, but the lines drawn, the shapes formed, and the colours chosen are what give the leader's life clarity.

How can a leader see with fresh eyes? Dramatist Lillian Hellman in her autobiography described the process as pentimento.[1] Historically when canvas was valuable and scarce, painters reused the canvas. They painted over the earlier works, particularly those they perceived as not their best work. Sometimes, faint traces of the old works would appear in some kinds of light. But it was the new work that was most visible, most real. As a metaphor for leadership, pentimento is a process of reconsidering, reshaping, recreating. Pentimento is a change of perceptual perspective, a seeing with fresh eyes and insight. Pentimento is required to make sense of the leader's complex world. The ability of the leader to expose their own blindspots, to see their environment with a beginner's mind, and to redraw their canvas will become more critical as we move forward.

Recent neuropsychological research suggests that leaders can improve the odds of operating in a volatile environment by using parts of their brain and minds more effectively by learning how to develop their "blank canvas" capacity – their capacity to sense and go with what emerges.[2] Leaders need to see possibilities as well as realities, and to see from multiple perspectives. We are understanding the complex human brain in new ways. The average human brain has one hundred billion to one thousand billion neurons, each of which makes one hundred to ten thousand connections with other neurons.[3] The number of synapses formed among these neurons is at least ten trillion, and the length of the axon cables forming the neuron circuit measures something like several hundred thousand miles.[4]

Although the brain is complex, it also has a remarkable ability to create new circuits, a phenomenon known as *plasticity*. This capacity for regeneration means that the cerebral wiring for our own store of knowledge and memories, which grows as we do, is as unique as a thumbprint. It also means that if one area of the brain is diminished in capacity, by a stroke for example, new circuits may be laid in another location to compensate, essentially rewiring a person's store of knowledge and memories.

BLANK CANVAS LEADERSHIP

The blank canvas metaphor functions in a wholly different way in that it engages discovery, exploration, and curiosity. It operates with a discovery process rather than a program, with perception rather than analysis. It doesn't rely primarily on expressing words; it does not have categories or think in terms of "either/or." The discovery process used in the blank canvas metaphor engages the nonconscious, essential for rapid learning and adaptation.

The disciplined practice of discovery and exploration activates the nonconscious, and develops sense-making capabilities. By developing the nonconscious mind, leaders are more capable of responding effectively, because we are less inclined to blindly follow the learned blueprint. Instead we become more open and receptive to a new future. The practices of nonconscious thinking can show leaders how to bypass the ever-vigilant blueprint program. We need leaders who can draw out the ability of their colleagues to articulate what they see and experience, question them and help them shape it into meaningful strategy, compel them to develop the skills of deeper thought and sustained attention that they lack, and validate their sense of discovery and ownership of what they find. Innocence and ignorance are a distinct advantage. It is through these qualities that we can frame the questions that will chart the steps of the new landscape or paradigm.

The discovery and exploration process used on the leadership blank canvas primarily utilizes methods from the world of the artist and psychologist. People in organizations often have strong blueprint competencies in practical, scientific, concrete, and analytical thinking. Contrary to popular belief, leadership does not require that we discard these competencies. As Ralph Stacey, director of the Complexity and Management Centre of the Business School at the University of Hertfordshire in the United Kingdom indicates, these competencies are valuable when the environment is certain and totally agreed upon.[5] What we do need to do, however, is to supplement these with some nonconscious and nonlinear tools more useful in complex environments where uncertainty and disagreements are high.

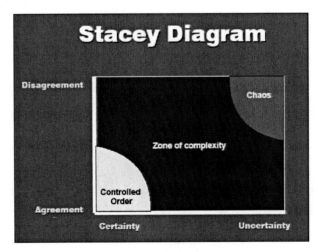

Figure 6-2: The Stacey Diagram: order and chaos.

CREATING RESTORATIVE MIND SPACE

How can leaders inspire their own dormant nonconscious thinking?

Leaders need to increase their capacity to voluntarily attend in an age of continuous partial attention. Leaders also need to diminish their inattentional blindness and overreliance on analytical/logical tools, and look at voluntary attention and unclutter their mind.

According to Mihaly Csikszentmihalyi, there is a tendency to focus voluntary attention too narrowly on ourselves, people, and things that give us material/emotional advantages.[6] Leaders operate in a world in which the boundary between quiet time or leisure time and business time is blurred, thanks to the capability of communications technology and the perceived need to stay connected. Today's business life, more likely than not, demands "24/7," as do some of the 24/7 personalities of the leaders who run many organizations. A survey by Christina Cavanagh, from the Richard Ivey School of Business at the University of Western Ontario shows that 45 percent of managers with heavy e-mail demands take laptops on vacation because they don't enjoy their holidays knowing that the messages are piling up.[7]

For many people, too little attention is left over to participate in the world on its own terms, to be surprised, to learn new things, to empathize, to grow beyond the limits set by our own self-centeredness, much like savants do.

> [Voluntary] attention is the most precious resource we have. Voluntary attention is more complex than a 'change,' a 'rest,' or 'diversions.' It is also more than eliminating 'distractions' and more than getting away from the familiar. How do we refresh our capacity to focus voluntary attention?

Giving full attention to a problem is not the best recipe for providing fresh perspectives and thoughts. We need to create safe external and internal environments for ourselves, our teams, organizations and societies that release voluntary attention.[8]

WHAT HELPS OUR CAPACITY TO VOLUNTARILY ATTEND?

Leaders need to develop intellectual humility and suspend judgment.

The German conductor Micael Andreas Gielen upon launching a new season of modern music once wrote a letter to potential subscribers. In it he conjured up a picture of "a guard standing at the threshold of perception" who would not allow modern music to enter because it was unusual and different. The maestro pointed out that most music lovers appreciate a Beethoven symphony because the form is familiar. And because it is familiar, the guards allow the music to enter. He went on to explain that we often reject modern music because our guards don't recognize the form and immediately turn away the music. Gielen warned, "unless the guardian is given the evening off... listeners might well miss the deepest emotional experiences offered by vital parts of the musical literature."[9] The unfamiliar can be surprisingly rewarding. To let nonconscious thinking emerge, fire the guards, or as my colleague Colin Funk director of creativity at the Banff Centre, states "Get rid of the gatekeeper," to establish openness and receptivity, and welcome new stimuli.[10]

Nonconscious thinking and talent exists within everyone. When people can't tap into their nonconscious, that doesn't mean that it's not there; it's just being suppressed by what Dr. Ray at Stanford University calls the "voice of judgment," or VOJ, which incessantly judges everything we do and holds us in a straight jacket.[11] Suspending judgment means a commitment to notice and to temporarily suspend our reactions, opinions, beliefs and assumptions. It is about being aware of our internal thoughts and putting them aside.

Judgment is a major inhibitor of responding to complexity. We are brought up in a world where judgment is the norm. We are not only quick to judge and criticize others, but have that so-called little 'voice of judgment' in our heads. We need to learn to withhold our judgment that says, I can't, we shouldn't, it can't happen, it doesn't make sense, it doesn't fit, and we're going to look stupid if we try. In the neurophenomenological studies of Francisco Varela, Jonathan Shear and Natalie Depraz, the authors note the processes used in focusing our voluntary attention: suspension, and letting go.[12] In order to see differently, leaders first have to suspend assumptions and let go and surrender to the moment.

DEVELOP A CURIOUS RESPONSE

Curiosity is the desire to know or the spark of interest that leads to exploration and discovery. Curiosity asks why things are the way they are and how they could be different. Rather than being passive receivers of sensory experiences, leaders are capable of receiving the world with fresh perceptions and acute awareness through both felt and imagined understandings. Leaders need to challenge themselves to wake up and observe the world anew, to see with fresh eyes. We are fed a substantial amount of data that potentially quashes curiosity. Leaders would do well to develop an awareness of wonderment, surrender, and attunement to enable curiosity.

How can a leader foster curiosity? The answer is to ask more questions, or as Rudyard Kipling once said "I keep six honest serving men, they taught me all I knew: their names are What and Why and When How and Where and Who."[13] Asking questions is the fundamental toolkit of journalists and children.

TRY THIS:

Write down ten questions that come to mind, things that you would love to know the answers to. Look through the questions and notice if any dominant themes emerge. Are there any areas of life that you seem most concerned with? Such as money, work, relationships, love, or health?

Nurturing a curious response to the world is simple and not easy. There are no ready-made maps. By nature, curiosity requires the unfamiliar, nonconventional, other frames of reference, engagement, and clarity of intention. Nurturing curiosity by dealing with an issue or challenge from a different angle allows us to generate new, different, and interesting ideas that can potentially help us out.

Frederick W. Smith, founder, chairman, president, and CEO of Federal Express says:

> There are two keys to (new thinking). The first is the ability to think beyond relatively conventional paradigms and to examine traditional constraints using nontraditional thinking. You have to be able to go outside your own frame of reference and find another way to look at a problem. The second key… is the ability to discern the important issues and to keep your real goal in view. Companies get into real trouble when they see a means as an end – when they fail to change their business processes: that's when some interloper comes along and does it for them.[14]

The process of curiosity thrives on diverse stimulation and a state of openness to experience. Leaders need and seek stimulation from different sources. What if leaders were to look at their environment as a hunt for treasure? Everywhere there would be clues to where the treasure is buried. But the leader needs to sift and probe, be alert and aware, and watch and question everything.

TRY THIS:

Use yourself as a blank canvas for sensing and bringing into the present that which wants to emerge. Move to a curious experimental mindset. Be in the world but not of it. Remind yourself to enjoy the journey, rather than obsess over the destination and lend your ears to music, open your eyes to painting, and above all stop thinking.

RETREAT AND REFLECT:
PROVIDE OPPORTUNITIES FOR "BEING TIME"

When you sit down to read a book, or to listen to a piece of music, or walk around an exhibition, without interruption the first thing you are doing is going inside the self. The demands and distractions of the world have to wait. As you draw your attention away from the world, you withdraw your energy from the world, and at that point, the creativity and concentration put into the making of the artwork begin to move into you. It's not simply about being re-charged, as in a good night's sleep or a holiday, it's about being recharged at a different voltage.

Art can uncover desires and appetites buried under the accumulating 24/7 emergency zones of our lives. Art can take the finger off the red panic button, and allow the heart rate to return to normal. Art suggests new possibilities. Time spent on art is free time in the truest sense. It is a moment when you don't belong to anyone. The moment when your time is your own, it is "being time."

What is being? Being is the connection between making sense and acting on it. Being makes it possible to go within yourself and allow nonconscious thinking to emerge. It is the space in which a leader achieves understanding through silence and reflection. Being is a source of energy and will. Being is essential for getting to the epiphanies that give leaders the knowledge of "elsewhere" that drives their vision.

The question is not "What are the appropriate actions?" it is "What is the appropriate being?" Being, may in fact, be a key to removing a critical impediment to leadership – obsessive focus on short-term results. Being gives us space for thinking differently and the ability to imagine emerging futures. *Without "being time," it is much more difficult for leaders to take a long-term view.*

How does one build being into leadership development programs? After an intense learning phase, leaders involved in our Innovation course at The Banff Centre spend time alone in the mountains to process and reflect on all that they have observed. They use this time to consider fresh perceptions and key learnings by keeping a journal. *Being* does not have to be so elaborate or extensive. An individual or group can find (or be alert to) small amounts of silence and reflection to facilitate learning and nonconscious thinking, and these times can have substantial impact. Quiet listening and stillness – or what aboriginal culture refers to as *dadirri* – has the ability to renew and refresh.[15] In stillness there is no need to reflect and do a lot of critical thinking. It is just about being aware and not being threatened by silence and just being at home in it.

Often, however, the perceived need for doing and busy-ness in organizational life makes silence and reflection a low priority, and it may not be regarded as a "safe" activity. Even in organizations where the value of being time is recognized, the press of urgent matters often pushes being time aside. We need to better understand the tools for being in order to assist leaders to engage in this important activity productively. Leaders need to create a safe environment inside themselves. Effective thinking endeavours do not depend solely on complex stimulating environments. Negative emotions such as sadness, fear, anxiety and boredom create "psychic entropy" and also must be minimized.[16] Why... concentration requires more effort when it goes against the grain of emotions and motivations. Attention is focused on restoring an inner subjective order, a forced reverie and relaxed knowingness. Like pianist Keith Jarrett, who clears his mind to engage in pure improvisation, a leader must learn to "overthrow the tyranny of the given, the known, the "right" way and create a space in tune with time and place.[17] Scharmer also describes this process of being as: a transformation of social space: decentering and collapsing social boundaries; a transformation of social time: slowing down to stillness; and ("self") and bringing into reality one's highest future potential ("self").[18]

SLOW DOWN YOUR THINKING: THETA BRAIN WAVES

The brain is an electrochemical organ; researchers have speculated that a fully functioning brain can generate as much as ten watts of electrical power.[19] Other more conservative investigators calculate that if all ten billion interconnected nerve cells discharged at one time, a single electrode placed on the human scalp would record something like five millionths to fifty millionths of a volt.[20] If you had enough scalps hooked up you might be able to light a flashlight bulb.

Even though the electrical power of the brain is very limited, it does occur in very specific ways. Electrical activity emanating from the brain is displayed in the form of brainwaves. According to neuropsychologists, there are four types of brainwaves that affect our thinking: beta, alpha, theta and delta. Accessing our nonconscious is more likely to occur during certain brain wave states.[21] When the brain is aroused and actively engaged in mental activities, it generates beta waves. These beta waves are relatively low amplitude, and are the fastest of the four different brainwaves. The frequency of beta waves ranges from fifteen to forty cycles per second.[22] Beta waves are characteristic of a strongly engaged mind. A person in active conversation would be in beta mode. A debater would be in high beta. A person making a speech, or a teacher, or a talk show host would all be in beta mode when they are engaged in their work.

The next brainwave category in order of frequency is alpha. Where beta represented arousal, alpha represents nonarousal. Alpha brainwaves are slower and higher in amplitude. Their frequency ranges from nine to fourteen cycles per second.[23] A person who has completed a task and sits down to rest is often in alpha mode. A person who takes time out to reflect is usually in alpha mode. A person who takes a break from a conference and walks in the garden is often in alpha mode.

The next brainwave state typically of even greater amplitude and slower frequency. Theta's frequency range is normally between five and eight cycles per second.[24] A person, who has taken time off from a task and begins to daydream is often in theta mode. A person, who is driving on a freeway and discovers that they can't recall the last five kilometres is often in theta mode – induced by the process of freeway driving. The monotonous nature of that form of driving compared to driving on a country road would differentiate a theta state and a beta state in order for the person to perform the driving task safely.

Individuals who do a lot of freeway driving often get good ideas during those periods; when they are in theta. Individuals who often run outdoors are in a state of mental relaxation that is slower than alpha and when in theta, they are prone to a flow of ideas. This can also occur in the shower or tub, or even while shaving or brushing your hair. Theta is a state where tasks become so automatic that you can mentally disengage from them. The ideation that can take place during the theta state is often free flow and occurs without censorship or guilt. It is during theta that leaders are more likely to access the nonconscious and develop new insights. It is typically a very positive mental state.

The final brainwave state is delta. Here the brainwaves are of the greatest amplitude and slowest frequency. They typically centre on a range of 1.5 to 4 cycles per second.[25] They never drop down to zero unless you are in a state of being brain dead. Outside of being brain dead, deep dreamless sleep would take you down to the lowest frequency, typically, two to three cycles a second.[26]

When we go to bed and read for a few minutes before attempting sleep, we are likely to be in low beta. When we put the book down, turn off the lights and close our eyes, our brainwaves will descend from beta to alpha to theta and finally, when we fall asleep, to delta. Being time and reflection both usually occurring in alpha and theta states, are critical to releasing nonconscious thinking and seeing in a new way.

TRY THIS:

Try keeping an idea journal so you can write down new ideas when they occur. Keep it with you at all times because you never know when you will get an idea. Thomas Edison had over 3,500 journals detailing his ideas, experiments, and patent applications when he died.[27] He continually reviewed them as a source for ideas.

You usually never know when an idea first comes whether or not it will amount to anything, so you should write all ideas your down as they come to you.

PAY ATTENTION AND NOTICE:
SITUATIONAL AWARENESS (SA)

Holmes, you see everything.

I see no more than you, but I have trained myself to notice what I see.[28]

Sherlock Holmes

The relationships between attention, awareness, and vision have yet to be clarified, but there is one thing about which most researchers agree: because we have a less than complete picture of the world at any one time, there is the potential for distortion and error (inattentional blindness). We usually take in no more than a handful of facts about the world. A million times more bits enter our heads than our consciousness perceives.[29] If leaders are not paying attention to some feature of the environment they won't see it. We are at the mercy of our change detection mechanisms. The danger according to Karl Weick is that "reliance on a single, uncontradicted data source can give people a feeling of omniscience, and skew their judgment and effectiveness."[30]

How do leaders evaluate a situation and decide if it is real and what to do about it? "It" is our perception of the situation and if "it" is generated by a self-image, we may deceive ourselves. Finally if "it" is generated by an information technology system, we may mistake that tapestry as real when the reality is something very different.

In order to help facilitate the understanding of what is out there, it is necessary to consider various questions and issues. For example; "What do (leaders) find relevant? How are they selective? How do they integrate new information with "old" social knowledge? How do they differentiate among messages? How perceptive are they of underlying messages?

So the question is this: how do leaders use their own observations to construct their pictures of reality and use these pictures to guide behaviour in a manner that serves them well and avoids inattentional blindness? Leaders can develop the ability to scan for signals about change and develop a readiness to move into new areas – and let go of the old ones, by observing and paying careful attention to what is in the environment. *When leaders take the blinders off they can see what is in front of them.* Sometimes it is necessary to get out of our own way to see what is ahead to know what's going on so we can figure out what to do effectively here and now in a specific situation that requires observing the world with fresh eyes.

IMMERSE YOURSELF

Critical to leadership is absorptive capacity, a term which describes the ability to recognize the value of new external information, assimilate it, and apply it.[31] It means immersing ourselves in environments that are relevant to our situation or quest by talking to different people, visiting unusual places, or reading about new subjects. It may also involve paying attention to things we are normally not aware of: activities we perform by rote, interactions we take for granted, expectations we've never questioned, or meanings we've never explored. The more we succeed in suspending our habits of judgment about what we notice and observe, the more clearly we will see what is going on around us. As a deeper way of seeing, sensing engages the imaginative mind as a tool for perception that will help us to see patterns, make new connections, and deepen our understanding of our world as it unfolds.

DEEP SITUATIONAL AWARENESS: FRAMING

How do we deal with the unexpected, the unknown, as well as recognizable situations? How do leaders effectively cope with information-rich situations where it is not known beforehand what is available in the environment, and the path to find the information is unknown? Information-rich also means that the information in the situation may change at any time. In order to respond effectively leaders need to develop deep situational awareness or DSA. Unrecognized patterns demand attention and require comprehension. The most effective leaders are likely to be those who in the words of W. Brian Arthur, Citibank Professor at Santa Fe Institute, "cognize" best – the people who can frame situations. As Arthur says;

> if you can figure out what the game is rather than how to play it – it's pretty obvious how to play it – then you're going to do well. If you think of the game as simply an extension of what went on before, you're going to get shoved out. There is a paradox, because if you are only inside the industry, you're used to what's being done already. So the idea is to be outside, to gather fresh recipes, fresh ingredients, learn new combinations, and then come back to your old position. But if you are in a pastry program and you're asked to do lamb, you're not going to get very far.[32]

WHAT IS DEEP SITUATIONAL UNDERSTANDING (DSU)?

DSU is comprised of: situational awareness and self-awareness. Mica Endsley of SA Technologies, defines situational awareness (SA) as the "perception of the elements in the environment within a volume of time and space, the comprehension of their meaning, and the projection of their status in the near future."[33] SA or the capacity to know what's going on in our current environment, what could happen next, what options we have for action, and what the possible outcomes of those actions might be. SA is an active process that directs the fluid allocation of attention and assessment of environmental cues.[34] The leader knows what's going on so they can figure out what to do. It is a dynamic mental representation of the current and future state of one's domain of action and includes awareness of the environment, entities, events, processes, actions and other's perceptions and intentions. It involves awareness of one's capacity to detect and interpret situational cues from multiple dynamically – changing data streams. It requires adaptation to an evolving situation, and tracking and utilizing special elements of knowledge.

WHAT KEY CAPACITY IS REQUIRED TO ENHANCE SA?

Leaders need to learn to be aware of how they think and perceive. This goes beyond mere awareness. It means leaders must become aware of their awareness. Metaperception and metacognition provide a subjective sense of awareness ("It's like looking over your own shoulder").

Metacognition is thinking about one's own thinking and metaperception is perceiving one's own perceptions. Both create an awareness of one's own SA. In accessing metacognition and metaperception one notices uncertainties, gaps, and potential conflicts in one's own perceptions and mental representations. Metacognition and metaperception allow one to assess one's ability to identify information needs and to employ strategies for sense-making and decision-making. Explicit sensing processes are needed when comprehension cannot easily occur. Explicit sensing requires metacognitive/perceptive awareness of one's own knowledge/perceptions and uncertainties, and gaps. Metacognitive assessments can be wrong and lead to inappropriate subjective attitudes and inappropriate behaviour.

Leaders need to ask the following questions to enhance their metacognitive capabilities.

1. How appropriate is my confidence in my situational awareness? Appropriate confidence is of course the ideal state. However, inappropriate confidence is the danger state.

2. How appropriate is my sensing capability? How confident am I in my ability to make sense of what is out there?

Other questions that measure SA are related to knowledge and processing:

Knowledge: would you say you have a good sense of:
the most recent information?
what is really going on?
what could happen?
what actions should be taken?

Processing: would you say it is easy for you to:
monitor the flow of information?
understand the big picture?
predict how it is likely to evolve?
decide what actions to take?

CARS, the Crew Awareness Ratings Scale, developed for U.S. Air Force pilot training, is a generic questionnaire that addresses both the mental content and mental processing of situational awareness with regard to four separate functions:

- perception: the assimilation of new information;
- comprehension: the understanding of information in context;
- projection: the anticipation of possible future developments;
- integration: the synthesis of the above with one's course of action.

For each of these four functional aspects, pilots are asked to rate:

- the content of that aspect: is it reliable and accurate?
- the processing of that aspect: is it easy to maintain?

The ratings for the questionnaire are given on a four - point scale ranging from the ideal case (1) to the worst case (4).[35]

Process Tips:

Leaders need to identify ways to help themselves and others handle unfamiliar situations. They need to:

- identify ways to help people know they are in unfamiliar situations;
- identify methods to notice and handle cues of low diagnosticity (pattern recognition);

- understand sensemaking at individual, group, organizational, and system levels;
- develop and use forcing scenarios as a method for analyzing the issues;
- develop a sensemaking framework;
- develop metrics for diagnosis and evaluation of sensemaking performance;
- understand the relationship between awareness, sensemaking and information;
- reconcile the differences between overlapping concepts (i.e., situational awareness, assessment, understanding, comprehension, mental maps, and sensemaking).

Sensemaking is about evaluating a situation and deciding if it is real, and what to do about it.

FURTHER DIAGNOSTIC QUESTIONS TO ASSESS SA

Can a picture of the situation be painted – a report on the conditions be made?

- Was enough of the "right" data collected and how was it collected?
- Was there correlational or contextual evidence of the data being put it together?
- Was the data put in a form that facilitates awareness?
- Was SA actually developed?
- Did the individuals involved develop appropriate SA?

- Was the SA shared with all who were involved?

- Was the situation correctly understood?

- Was sense made of the situation?[36]

HOW CAN LEADERS INCREASE SA?

1. Pay attention and engage acute observation:

    - purposefully set out to notice things or just pause when things happen by chance;

    - explicitly assign a meaning to an episode;

    - record thoughts so you won't forget them.

2. Bring together people with different eyes, different lenses, and different voices:

    - read and absorb material from many different fields and genres;

    - talk to strangers;

    - listen intently, seek to understand the other person's mental constructs;

    - purposely try to think like someone else;

    - engage in role-plays; they can yield innovative insights.

3. Engage mindfulness:

    - ask questions: who, what, when, where, why, and how, but resist the urge to answer too quickly;

- ask juicy questions;

- practice multimode thinking;

- don't overlook the obvious, list what is right in front of you;

- make a list of assumptions, paradigms, and rules;

- look for patterns in an industry to spot opportunities for innovation;

- take literal and imaginative excursions.

4. Paint new canvases:

- construct a detailed picture of a new world, and then walk around in it;

- separate environmental factors into those that you feel are reasonably predictable and those which are uncertain;

- create environmental scenarios by holding the predictable factors steady and randomly modifying the uncertain factors;

- create idealized competitors, customers, employees, or technologies, anything that provides innovative escape will help;

- constructing scenarios is an art, there is no way to know which scenarios will generate the most innovative ideas; simply go for a maximum variety of two to four cases;

- blend your innovative and analytical skills to generate plausible but imaginative scenarios (or assemble a team with a good mix).

TRY THIS:

Metacognize and think about your own thinking. Al Andrade, of Harvard's Cognitive Skills Group, suggests "One Minute Papers," a short exercise which provides leaders with an opportunity to step back and think about their thinking.[37] Thinking about thinking often is a neglected and yet vital part of the leadership process. Reflection allows leaders to pause and assess not only the product of their thinking but also the quality of the thinking itself.

Directions:

Take a moment to think about the thinking you just did. Then answer the following questions:

- what new ideas, questions, insights, puzzles, or connections did you have?
- what was effective about the thinking you did?
- what could have been better?
- what will you do next time to improve your thinking?

When to use One Minute Papers

One minute papers can be used as a thinking activity after completing a project or during a meeting as an ongoing assessment check; during the introduction of a new or complex topic as an ongoing assessment check; or at any point where you want participants to be aware and take stock of their thinking.

How to use One Minute papers

One minute papers can be used:

- as a tool to introduce leaders and team members to the concept of mental management and reflection;

- as a learning tool to help leaders and team members identify patterns (both strong and weak) in their thinking over time;

- as a communication tool to help leaders and team members articulate their thinking processes;

- as an assessment tool for leaders to help team members set standards for effective thinking.[38]

PHYSICAL SPACE

In addition to getting brain space to centre voluntary attention, creating an appropriate physical space is crucial for the nonconscious to flourish. John Kao, the author of *Jamming: The Art and Discipline of Business Creativity*, maintains that innovation happens in places and spaces, noting that artists have studios for a reason. He says:

There are all kinds of ceremonial elements to make sure people know that there's a distinction between ordinary life and the innovative environment where the work goes on. That is why I think the architecture of innovation is going to change dramatically over the next five to ten years. There are quite a few companies that are interested in having some kind of a corporate think space or quiet space or slow space where new things can happen. Nobody's figured out the architectural principles. A lot of companies are fiddling around with that. But five to ten years from now, it'll be a more commonly understood need and people will have more ways of practicing innovation that are, if not standardized, at least recognized: we need that. We need our Idea Factory, opening the mind and allowing the sparks to emerge.[39]

WHAT KINDS OF PHYSICAL ENVIRONMENTS HAVE RESTORATIVE POTENTIAL?

The following list describes the characteristics of restorative space.

1. It will provide a *sense of being away* (nature's quietness) not merely escape or withdrawal (which could be confining or boring). It is an environment that could be free from sensory distractions, or one that is comprised of elements of natural, exotic, or remote elements.

2. It will provide *fascination*, for it is with fascination that we experience attention that is effortless. The environment will allow one to rest the mental activities associated with the pressures and strains of the everyday world. This fascinating environment can be fascinating in its process or content. It can be a place that is strange and exotic. Cities are attractive because of their atmosphere of excitement, freedom, and creativity. According to Mihaly Csikszentmihalyi people report their most positive involuntary attention experiences in public spaces, surrounded by strangers, parks, streets, restaurants, theatres, clubs, and beaches.[40]

3. It will be an environment designed to "hang together" or it will have *coherence and consistency* thereby creating an interconnected positive experience.[41]

TRY THIS:

Create a corporate think space or quiet space or slow space where new things can happen.

SUMMARY OF CREATING RESTORATIVE SPACE

Creating restorative space is preparation and can lead naturally into nonconscious thinking and the development of imaginative ideas.

- Leaders need to learn how to create restorative space (both brain and physical). The lack of brain space is a major reason why opportunities are frequently missed.

- Uncluttering the brain and creating spaces are an essential part of the leadership process.

- Creating restorative paces needs to occur frequently as we live our lives in a complex and uncertain world.

- Creating restorative space is also deliberate; one can sit down and do it. It is immediate, it is in the here and now.

- Creating restorative space is about expansive thinking. The goal is to identify more available mental and perceptual valleys than when one began.

Leaders need to be more deliberate about breaking free from continuous partial attention in order to get their bearings. It is difficult to execute well while looking for the next best thing to sync up to. Speed is not the only answer to today's business challenges. The key in a volatile environment is pausing to reflect, noticing where attention is focused, thinking a challenge through; and then taking steady steps forward in an intentional manner. The tools to assist in this process are described in the next two chapters.

7

CHAPTER SEVEN:
THE NEW LEADERSHIP SENSING TOOLBOX
PART ONE

PART ONE:
VISUAL PRACTICES FOR A NEW LEADERSHIP ERA

If you want to change how people think, give them a tool the use of which will lead them to think differently.
Buckminster Fuller

Figure 7-1: The Image Explorer - Heemsbergen Sensory Awareness Tools (H-SAT)

We need to probe beneath the surface to reveal, *what leaders don't know they know.* Because approximately 95 percent of all thought occurs in the nonconscious, traditional leadership practices, which focus on conscious thinking, miss much of the mark.

THE VISUAL APPROACH

Leaders think in images and metaphors. An exploration of metaphoric tools from the world of art and psychology can provide a fresh context and can assist in the process of developing new leadership by uncovering the nonconscious mind of leaders and their employees. The visual approach recognizes that leaders think and communicate in complex ways that blueprint methods do not capture.

The visual approach uses various means to elicit information from leaders, with an emphasis on visual images, metaphors, and multisensory experiences. The use of metaphors can uncover profound information about leadership, clients, vendors, employees, suppliers, customers, and what truly inspires their decisions. All of this is difficult to access with any other research tools.

Each tool in the visual approach is designed to trigger different structures and sense modalities in the brain, whether visual, kinesthetic, or language-based. With the visual approach leaders are guided through imagery and other nonverbal methods to develop a nonconscious vocabulary. When leaders start activating their nonconcious brains, a powerful richness and diversity emerges that overshadows the traditional verbal methods of asking questions.

METAPHORS

Metaphor is the engine of imagination.
Gerald Zaltman

The word "metaphor" comes from the Greek word *metapherein*, which means to transfer or to change. Poets and psychologists understand that metaphor - viewing one thing in terms of another - is key to understanding our thinking and crucial to uncovering nonconscious needs and emotions. A metaphor can transform an intangible idea into an image that people can more easily grasp. It can also provide accurate diagnostic information that can stimulate creative action. Today metaphors frequently used in organizations are related to the military or sports ("War on talent," "Make sure you hit the ball," "We have to get the puck the net"). The Disney Corporation uses theatre or show metaphors. In the show metaphor, employees are "cast members" (not employees), they "wear costumes" (not uniforms); they play their "roles" (not jobs) to "guests" (not consumers). In contrast, the predominant metaphors in use in organizations today are those of machine and military operations.

The metaphor is an important thinking and diagnostic tool to gain insights into leadership practice by tapping into the nonconscious mind. Metaphor is more appealing than pure rhetoric or words because it stimulates the imagination and appeals to emotions. *Through metaphors, it is possible to make sense of a complex world by drawing out certain characteristics. At the same time, metaphors allow for diverse (ambiguous) and multiple interpretations and perspectives.* Yet many leaders are so caught up in the literal that they neglect the metaphoric or they use readily accessible metaphors from old paradigms.

Are there other metaphors, which may be more suited to today's complex and volatile environment? Thia von Ghyczy, director of business projects at the Darden School of Business, at the University of Virginia, makes a distinction between *rhetorical metaphors and cognitive metaphors.*[1] The former are deemed as dead metaphors, in that they offer little in the way of new perspectives and insights. Many military and sports metaphors fall into this category because they only offer familiarity. However, cognitive metaphors as von Ghyczy describes them are meant to aid in the discovery of learning. These metaphors are not immediately clear "in fact they should startle and puzzle us."[2] The richness of the cognitive metaphor "lies in the richness and rigor of debate it engenders."[3] Leaders need to provide cognitive metaphors to open up ideas and stimulate thinking.

ARTISTIC METAPHORS

The arts have recently inspired a growing use of metaphors in organizations. For example, musical metaphors have been used in relation to teamwork ("jamming"), organizations ("improvisation"), and leadership ("band leadership").[4]

These relatively new metaphors are able to stimulate the imagination, and empower and explain complexity. These metaphors are only new in that they have not been widely used before, despite the fact that everyone has access to them.

ACCESSIBILITY OF METAPHORS

Metaphors help people make sense of their everyday experiences. Metaphors have the tremendous advantage of being grounded in what is familiar, often at an intuitive and nonconscious level. As such, not only do they facilitate rapid comprehension, they often suggest new dimensions to what is being conveyed through them. These unforeseen dimensions can provide subtle poetic linkages between isolated mechanistic concepts, as well as totally new insights to be explored. We need to apply new models and metaphors for effective leadership. We need new images and metaphors for the future.

TRY THIS:

Create a metaphor for an issue or challenge to understand and make sense of it. For example the challenge could be described as a journey.

- Different types of metaphors leaders can use include:
- direct metaphor: look at similar forms and functions in related systems;
- personal metaphor; use personal experience;
- symbolic metaphor: look at similar forms and function in unrelated systems;
- fantasy metaphor: indulge your imagination.

IMAGINIZATION

Gareth Morgan from the Schulich School of Business at York University introduced the term and process of "imaginization" as a way to break free from habits of the mind and heart into space that allows for acting differently. Morgan views metaphor as the primary means through which we forge our relationship to the world. According to Morgan, the images we hold of the world and ourselves can either constrain or expand our potential for transformation.[5] By developing an image of an organizational structure, a problem area, or the future, we can gain insight into how our organization operates and what it will take to make necessary changes. Nature supplies many excellent ideas for imaging. For example, we might imagine an organization as an ant colony, a river, or a spider's web. Morgan's ideas about imaginization could also lead one to think about conceiving of an organizational change initiative by using images of ships, seas, winds, and icebergs.[6]

INNOVATIVE VISUALIZATION –
A PICTURE IS WORTH A THOUSAND WORDS

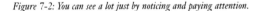

Figure 7-2: You can see a lot just by noticing and paying attention.

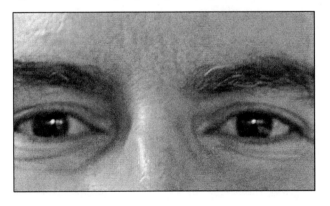

The leader's nonconscious mind, the most powerful portion of the brain, sees things primarily in pictures. It does not see in words of any language. We "see" at our nonconscious neuron level in pictures. Furthermore, our nonconscious neurons do not have the reality, rational thinking, and reasoning filters that are present in our conscious neurons. And since these pictures are filterless, we are not able at the nonconscious level to see the deductively reasoned picture that we "see" at the conscious level.

J.E. LeDoux, in his book *The Emotional Brain*, reports that certain impulses received by our eyes are sent directly to the amygdala (seat of emotions) instead of to the cortex for further interpretation, analysis, and decision-making.[7] The determining factors that decide which impulses are sent directly to the amygdala and which go to the cortex seem to be based on several factors. If the impulse images are related to any fear or danger producing past images for an individual, they go directly to the amygdala for quick attention and response. Images and impulses for things of great importance to us, are likewise sent to the amygdala for direct, immediate focus, action and attention.

What leaders do is a product of both the cortex (conscious brain) and the nonconscious functions (sensing and memories). In an increasingly technological environment, the ability to perceive, interpret, understand, and evaluate sensory data is critical. The visual arts world supports the development of multiple capabilities that allow leaders to understand and decipher an increasing variety of images and symbols. Susanne Langer, an American philosopher, has said that the visual arts are the objectification of feeling, developing intuition and teaching the eye to perceive expressive form.[8]

Leaders need to engage the mind's eye through visual images to see and influence the future as it emerges, to see all there is to see and relearn the art of seeing. Visual thinking is an essential skill for the leader. It engages leaders in a process of observing, investigating, and interpreting what they see in a picture, thereby enhancing their ability to think visually and communicate ideas in visual ways. If we open our eyes and notice, we give our attention to that which is beyond ourselves but present.

In everyday life and in learning, visual information is used to interpret experience and build understanding. This fact can be illustrated in three ways. First, visual thinking is part of the way we reason, such as when we extract information from a map, chart, or table and represent and express it in language. Second, visual thinking can be integral to problem-solving, such as when we need to use a diagram to explain, document, calculate or show the steps involved in reaching a solution. Third, visual representation can play a role in communication, for instance such as when one uses diagrammatic and visual forms to communicate information, represent data, and show relationships.

Both visual and verbal experiences support knowledge construction, and a great deal of sensory learning is visual.[9] It has been estimated that approximately fifty to seventy-five percent of our brains are comprised of neurons devoted to processing visual stimuli.[10] On these grounds, opportunities should be sought in leadership environments to exploit the visual mode of expression and thinking.

The visual representation of ideas is just as much a part of the leadership process as using language and other symbolic representations, yet current theories of leadership do not always highlight this important dimension of the decision-making process. To what extent does current leadership practice utilize visual resources to enable individuals to learn more effectively?

TRY THIS:
Visual learning techniques

- look more closely and analyze what you see;

- when in doubt, draw a picture or ask someone to draw a picture;

- borrow concepts from other forms of communication (such as film, comics etc.);

- start an idea log.

Through images, leaders can more capably clarify their thinking, and make sense and meaning out of complexity. Visualization can assist leaders in seeing how ideas are connected and it helps them recognize how information can be grouped or organized. With visualization, new data and information can be more thoroughly and easily understood. Visual diagrams reveal patterns, interrelationships, and interdependencies. They also stimulate innovative thinking.

Visualization reinforces understanding. We recreate in our own words what we've learned through the power of images and this enables us to absorb and internalize new information.

Visualization also integrates new knowledge. Diagrams prompt leaders to build upon prior knowledge and internalize new information. By reviewing diagrams, we can see how facts and ideas fit together.

Sara Diamond, artistic director of media and visual arts at the Banff Centre, Alberta, Canada, states, "visualization is one of the most common devices we use to understand information. Studying a map helps us understand our location and the layout of our surroundings. Examining charts and graphs helps us organize statistics better than simply reading the figures. Cookbooks use pictures to complement their recipes."[11]

Visualization techniques are powerful sense-making tools that support knowledge workers in their decision-making activities by stimulating visual thinking. In today's technology and data-oriented world, businesses have managed to amass more corporate data than they can analyze. Data visualization provides the capabilities to extract meaningful information from large stores of data, and thus it will emerge as a leading business-data-analytical solution in the coming years.[12] Data visualization technology is well suited to analyzing large and complex datasets.

In recent years, corporate information processing power, the advent and growth of e-commerce, and business presence on the Internet have resulted in organizations having unprecedented amounts of data concerning their customers, their business transactions, and their business processes. Web-based businesses have mechanisms to gather unprecedented amounts of data concerning their customers, sales, and business processes.[13] According to Charles Wang, CEO of the Computer Associates Company in Islandia, New York, businesses "have more data than they know what to do with, but don't have the necessary tools to aggregate that data into intelligent business information."[14] In order to gain useful information from this data one must derive relationships, patterns, or trends from the data. Data visualization is proving to be a key technology in successfully analyzing data, and will therefore be highly demanded by businesses in the near future.

WHAT TYPES OF VISUAL TOOLS ARE AVAILABLE TO LEADERS?

Leaders can turn almost any object within reach into a tool for visualization or imaginization to access nonconscious thinking. Writers use notes to trigger imagery. Sketches, doodlings, and jottings are other ways to note down thoughts that can later be expanded. Personal organizers such as PalmPilots and software idea generators also have the potential to support nonconscious thinking.

Seemingly independent visual or mental images that are considered concurrently may also inspire unique ideas. According to his own story (which contradicts the story of being hit on the head by a falling apple), Sir Isaac Newton conceived the concept of universal gravitation when he observed an apple falling and at the same time noticed the moon in the sky. These simultaneous images inspired him to speculate that the same laws governed the falling apple and the moon orbiting the earth. This in turn led him to develop the laws of mechanics, and establish mathematical analysis and modeling as the principal foundations of science and engineering. Newton's Laws were inspired by a combination of visual images.

THE VISUAL TOOLKIT –
HOW LEADERS CAN THINK VISUALLY

How can leaders assess their own visual potential and develop techniques and strategies to make sense of the environment? The following section explains a wide range of visual tool techniques and processes leaders can use to come up with creative and imaginative solutions to the challenges they face.

Mindscape

Nancy Margulies, who contributed a chapter on visual mapping in Joyce Wyckoff and Tim Richardson's book, *Transformation Thinking*, offers a unique innovative visualization exercise that can assist in utilizing more of the brain's nonconscious capacity.[15] Rather than writing out a list of thoughts and ideas about a goal, Margulies recommends drawing a "mindscape" of it – a simple drawing that represents its various aspects in pictures instead of words. Mindscapes encourage individuals to find visual metaphors for situations – goals can be shown at the end of a road or in clouds overhead. Margulies concludes, "We can depict roadblocks, possible dead ends, bridges, sidetracks and other challenges of journeying toward a goal."[16]

Once, Margulies asked executives at a major chemical company to each draw a Mindscape depicting a major objective reached at some time in their careers, using a hike to the top of a mountain as the setting – a "Trek Mindscape" as she called it.[17] This visual model helped the executives acknowledge past successes in their lives and identify the types of resources they used and the barriers they overcame.

If one is able to doodle, compelling mindscapes are possible. The goal is not to create a work of art, but to get the brain to reveal something at a nonconscious level about a past success or current objective using visual metaphors. While drawing the shapes and symbols for the various elements in the mindscape, it is important to leave room within them, to draw one or two lines next to them, where a few words can be written describing what each shape or symbol means.[18]

THE CUBE

At the Idea Factory in San Francisco and Singapore, John Kao also utilized visualization tools. He says:

One of the big things we do is to use visual tools to try to move thinking away from verbal, analytical thinking alone to more analogy – based, inductive, and visual kinds of thinking. We may do an exercise in the beginning that captures some of that flavor. We invented a tool that uses photos you can attach to a cube. It's like a visual Rorschach test of social issues and elements that make up our world. The scripting of this exercise depends on the client, but we might say something like, introduce yourself and tell us what you're most concerned about, and select three or four images that tell that story.[19]

Reflection and visualization also provided inspiration to Philo Farnsworth, which led to the invention of the television. While sitting on a hillside in Idaho, Farnsworth observed the neat plowed rows of dirt made by his uncle's horse-drawn harrow on the farm. This gave him the idea of creating a picture on a cathode ray tube made out of rows of light and dark dots. He was fourteen at the time. The next year he presented the concept as a high-school science project.[20]

VISUAL EXPLORER

About Learning, Inc. an educational products firm has developed a tool called Visual Explorer, a collection of over three hundred high-quality images, photographs, and paintings that help teachers connect to students learning in new and innovative ways.[21] Visual Explorer is an experiential tool that uses visual images and metaphors to enable students to make connections across multiple disciplines, use images as building blocks to achieve higher levels of understanding and dialogue and to see patterns and relationships among ideas and discuss opinions, viewpoints, and perspectives.

Virtually any choice made with a task in mind allows leaders to project their thoughts and feelings onto the image, resulting in rich discussions not captured by verbal methods. Responses to images vividly tap the nonconscious brain and many times, surprisingly. For example, Charles J. Palus and David M. Horth also use 204 carefully chosen colour images, in a kit also entitled Visual Explorer to invite examination and encourage conversation at the Centre for Creative Leadership (CCL) in Greensboro, North Carolina.[22] In typical usage, participants are asked to select an image (while browsing the entire set) that evokes for them some important aspect of the previously defined challenge (or issue, idea, etc.) of which the group has tried to make sense. Dialogue then proceeds in small groups with leaders describing their challenge and sharing their perceptions and impressions with others.

Conventional approaches to developing, capturing, manipulating, and reusing information and knowledge, while still valuable, don't provide enough support, especially at the pressure points – those points where everyday sensemaking fails.[23] Visual Explorer provides leaders an opportunity to explore their own metaphors and tap their nonconscious brain by selecting images. Leaders project their own thoughts, motivations, desires, and feelings, and so on onto the image chosen. The inner world of the leader's brain, thoughts, and desires stirs up the dynamic of projection on two levels, the sensory and the psychological. On the sensory level: the mind synthesizes sensory experiences (sight, hearing, smell, taste, touch) and produces a composite picture, which is then projected onto the external environment, creating the appearance of a world "out there."

On the psychological level, leaders project their thoughts, feelings and memories onto the sensory world, thereby creating their own unique experience, the nonconscious formation of conscious information.

TRY THIS:

Select from a group of photos or magazine pictures an image that speaks to you about your sense of purpose in your leadership, and jot down some notes describing what comes to mind. It doesn't take great visual talent to describe a concept through pictures. Pay attention to your expressive impulse. Choose an image that depicts effective teamwork and pick another one depicting a dysfunctional team.

Select another image that represents what your organization/ team might look like in five years.

Drawing: Another Tool in the Doctor's Bag?

Drawing also enables leaders to visualize or see what they are thinking and saying. Drawing invokes our nonconscious thinking and provides greater clarity. Everybody knows how to draw, doodle, or scribble. In a recent experiment, children with headache pain who visited their physicians were asked to draw a picture of themselves and what their pain felt like. The children's drawings of their headache pain clearly enabled the doctors to diagnose the difference between migraine and nonmigraine headaches. [24]

If Words Aren't Enough Show Me

Pictures fill in the conceptual void when words fail to express what we are trying to relate. In his book, *Art is Work*, Milton Glaser, who has been a seminal figure in graphic design for more than fifty years, says, "The act of drawing has nothing to do with being an illustrator. We draw because it enables us to see... drawing is the path to observation and attentiveness."[25] Leaders frequently encounter situations where they are unable to absorb and comprehend all of the necessary information discussed at a meeting. Nate Burgos, a Chicago-based design manager, states, "If you could only see what was being said. If you could only see the criteria being addressed. If you could only see the ideas being relayed."[26] Drawing allows the leader to "see" and enables movement between what is and what could be. Burgos says, "With a few quick strokes, you can capture multiple views of a concept and crystallize possible solutions. Drawing is conversation of minds over matter: you can see what is being thought and said."[27]

TRY THIS:

- Doodle as you think about a problem. Generate three or four pictures. Depict attributes or options as graphic symbols. Draw each symbol on a separate card. Mix and match the cards to generate potential solutions (i.e. story boards).

- Try brainsketching in which each individual sketches out a potential solution to the challenge presented. Then each sketch is passed on to another person who modifies it. After a specified number of passes, the sketches are collected and examined.

New leadership in unpredictable times needs to be not only decisive and strategic, but must also incorporate sensing to create context, and recognize patterns and understand that which cannot yet be seen. Drawing can facilitate this sense and meaning-making. As part of a leader's skill set, drawing demonstrates what matters and what makes sense. Drawing literally draws out the leader and their colleagues in their thinking about a need or challenge. As Nick Burgos states, "In so doing, insight and discovery increase the intellectual depth of the collaboration. Such communication resonates with purpose, community, and inventiveness. Drawing enables anyone to make visible their imaginings and sustain them so all will be led on a journey of realization – locally and globally."[28] Drawing according to Burgos:

- authenticates conceptualization;

- drives discussion and participation;

- enables exploration and insight;

- simplifies what we comprehend;

- can break down barriers, simplifies what we comprehend;

- ushers in effective discourse;

- is highly plastic, and can adapt to the climate of the room;

- has the power to unite diverse people;

- engages spontaneity;

- and enables "what if" questions (facts opinion, nature, the media).[29]

TRY THIS:

Create a canvas.

The physical environment can be conducive to self-expression and cocreation. Encourage the utilization of any available surface in the office for drawing and doodling - Post-it notes, flipcharts, whiteboards, lunch napkins. The more surfaces you have for mental maneuvering the better.

TRY THIS:

Nondominant hand drawing.

Letting your nondominant hand draw is also a way to let go and let your nonconscious thinking emerge. It is more likely that the nondominant hand is going to go to where it wants, rather than be controlled. The "Upside Down Picasso" exercise is frequently used as a way of illustrating the importance of drawing. In it, participants copy a Picasso drawing of Stravinsky by turning it upside down, covering the image with a piece of paper, then uncovering the first eighth of an inch or so, drawing a few visible lines, uncovering the next eighth of an inch and carefully adding that now visible bit of detail, and so on. The gradual unfolding requires time, attention, and discipline. The exercise, though onerous, can yield insights about the necessity of focus on process rather than outcome, and it can also untap potential drawing talent.[30]

WHAT IS CONCEPT MAPPING?

Concept mapping is another visual tool for representing knowledge in graphs. Knowledge graphs are networks of concepts. Networks consist of nodes (points/vertices) and links (arcs/edges).[31] Nodes represent concepts and links represent the relations between concepts.[32]

Concept mapping can be done for several purposes:

- to generate ideas;
- to design a complex structure (long texts, large web sites);
- to communicate complex ideas;
- to aid learning by explicitly integrating new and old knowledge;
- to assess understanding or diagnose misunderstanding.

Prof. Joseph D. Novak at Cornell University developed the concept mapping technique. Novak concluded, "meaningful learning involves the assimilation of new concepts and propositions into existing cognitive structures."[33]

HOW ARE MIND MAPS CREATED?

Mind mapping is a popular technique related to concept mapping, invented (and copyrighted) by Tony Buzan in the United Kingdom. Buzan says, "a mind map consists of a central word or concept, around the central word you draw the 5 to 10 main ideas that relate to that word. You then take each of those words and again draw the 5 to 10 main ideas that relate to each of those words."[34] By focusing on key ideas written down in their own words, and then looking for branches and connections between the ideas, leaders can map knowledge in a manner to help them understand and remember new information. The important thing to remember when creating a mind map is to draw quickly without pausing, judging or editing.

The difference between concept maps and mind maps is that a mind map has only one main concept, while a concept map may have several. This comes down to the point that a mind map can be represented as a tree, while a concept map may need a network representation.

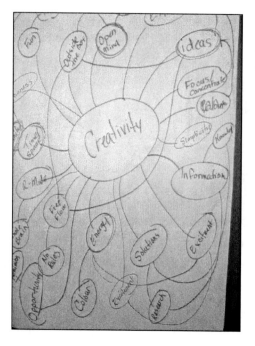

Figure 7-3: Example of a Mind Map of Creativity

WHAT IS CLUSTERING?

Another visual tool to support thinking and to tap the nonconscious was developed by Gabriele Rico, author of the book *Writing the Natural Way*. The tool Rico developed is called clustering which can be used to generate ideas for any business challenge.[35]

With clustering, leaders are requested to write and circle a central topic, in the centre of a page, and to fill the whole page with their ideas each circled and linked, working quickly without censoring any ideas that may come. Only at the end of the exercise are leaders asked to look over their work, cross out ideas that are irrelevant or not useful, and then number the ideas in the order they wish to discuss them. They may then create a formal outline. Leaders can begin with a single word representing a challenge, circle the word in the centre of a blank page, then as quickly as possible, create a cluster of words or ideas, each circled and linked back to the centre word or word preceding it.

ZALTMAN METAPHOR ELICITATION TOOL (ZMET)

The first patented marketing research tool in the United States, ZMET relies on visual images to uncover people's preferences and hidden thoughts about the products and services they use. For example, customers are asked a question about a particular product and then requested to spend a week finding pictures that express their feelings and thoughts about using that product. They then discuss the images during a two-hour private interview with a ZMET specialist. Finally, they create a digital collage with their images and record a short text about its meaning. The ZMET's defining characteristic is the use of metaphor to elicit consumer's nonconscious attitudes toward particular products and brands. "Metaphors are essential to how we think, they're essential for us to understand what is said to us, and they're essential for how we process that information," explains ZMET architect Gerald Zaltman. "It's essential for how we represent to other people what we think, how we feel, why we do what we do."[36]

TRY THIS:

Divide a team into three groups and assign each group a specific product/process or service to analyze. Next, ask each team member to clip out magazine pictures and to assemble them into a collage that will then serve as a metaphor for experiences and emotions associated with the product/process or service. After a period of time, each team member will present their collage and will be allotted several minutes to display it while they explain why they chose certain clippings and what the clippings mean. In the next phase, each group will meet to interpret the metaphorical meanings within the stories. The final task of each team is to produce a paper detailing product/process or service uses, consumer preferences and dislikes, and opportunities and threats.

I CAN SEE CLEARLY NOW, THE BRAIN IS GONE

In addition to more traditional analytical tools used, leaders need to use their eyes, to notice hidden or unseen things that tell them what is really going on and to see what's in front of their eyes, rather than what their conceptual minds think they're seeing. The eye of the leader does not usually see what is actually there because the narrative-trained mind overrides the eyes. Leaders don't usually see with their eyes, they see with their programmed mindsets. The power of acute visual observation, to notice and pay attention is one of the most useful tools to start making sense of what wants to emerge in the environment.

Using visual tools and methods, leaders are also able to learn what makes them and their colleagues/team members tick from the inside out. By engaging visual tools, leaders can get a clear focus on who they are, what they want, where they're going, and how to get there. Visual tools are able tap the nonconscious brain and uncover hidden meanings and talents.

8

CHAPTER EIGHT:
THE NEW LEADERSHIP SENSING TOOLBOX
PART TWO

PART TWO:
MOVEMENT AND SOUND PRACTICES FOR A
NEW LEADERSHIP ERA

In addition to the tools of visualization discussed in the last chapter, leaders can learn from using the tools of movement and sound. The movement and sound approaches similarly recognize that leaders think and communicate in complex ways that traditional methods do not capture. The movement and sound approaches use various means to elicit information from leaders and team members, with an emphasis on improvisation, narrative, listening, sculpting, and acting.

One of the overarching tools is improvisation, which can be used in movement and sound. By engaging in exercises that encourage spontaneity and fresh thinking, leaders learn a different "way" to approach challenges and solve problems "on their feet."

WHAT CAN IMPROVISATION TEACH LEADERS?

John Kao writes:

In today's global marketplace there's no time for business managers to look for solutions in the archives of corporate sheet music. Our highly competitive business world puts a premium on the skill of improvisation. All the world's a jazz club. This is an era, in short, that calls for the inspiration of art. The innovative role of the manager is to work the central paradox, or tension, of the jam session: to locate the ever-mobile sweet spot somewhere between systems and analysis on the one hand and the free-flowing creativity of the individual on the other.[1]

WHAT IS IMPROVISATION?

The word "improvisation" derives from *"improvisus,"* Latin for "not seen ahead of time." Improvising involves behaving, acting, or playing extemporaneously, without a script. Stephen Leybourne of Plymouth Business School in the United Kingdom, (quoting Gilbert Ryle a former editor of the journal *Mind*), describes improvisation as the pitting of an acquired competence or skill against unprogrammed opportunity, obstacle or hazard. It is not merely composing on the fly or making it up as you go.[2] It is leadership that follows recipes rather than blueprints. "Improvisation is the conception of action as it unfolds, drawing on available material, cognitive, affective and social resources."[3] It is to spontaneously recombine what you know. The competencies needed to be effective at improvisation are quickness and agility, the ability to take risks, good listening, and the ability to build on the work of others.

Karl Weick talks about *bricolage*, a French word that does not translate easily.[4] Bricolage is a form of improvisation practiced by some, which uses whatever resources and repertoire that come to hand in order to perform an immediate task. A person who practices bricolage is called a <u>bricoleur</u>. A bricoleur is a person who can routinely make what they need from what is at hand.[5] For example, they can make a uniquely useful machine from spare parts in a barn and it may do the job better than anything on the market. In a paper called "Organizational Redesign as Improvisation," Weick identifies the following requirements for successful bricolage:

- intimate knowledge of resources;
- careful observation and listening;
- trusting one's ideas;
- self-correcting structures, with feedback.[6]

Improvisation is an idea that is related to bricolage. It is quite different from experimentation in that it helps to root learnings that are highly transferable to other forms of behaviour in organizations.

Free improvisation basically means starting out with a blank canvas: not having any idea what notes/scenes/patterns/ideas you are about to see/hear/record or play. As a genre, it refers to jazz artists, breaking out of the structure of chord changes and/or rhythmic tradition.

Jazz improvisation involves moving beyond standard routines and formalizations to create music on the spot without a prescribed score or plan. However, it is also guided by a non-negotiable framework, which constrains what the soloist can play.

In the context of leadership, it can be viewed as a contributor to and an outcome of the capacity for new knowledge, market flexibility, entrepreneurial culture, and innovation. "Jamming" is a dynamic and iterative process of constructing, performing, and adjusting ideas as a result of close contact with an employee, audience, client, learner, or customer.

Like a musical jam session, improvisational jamming follows a recipe rather than a blueprint. By giving attention to the phenomena of musical improvisation as an art form of depth, expression, reflection, sheer abandon, digging into the deep void of the mystery of our life's existence, musical improvisation can give us a technique for a deeper human connection with the source of our nonconscious mind.[7] Its practice and appreciation may facilitate a greater leadership consciousness.

Figure 8-1: Theatre Improvisation at the Banff Centre.

According to Frank J. Barrett, from the Naval Postgraduate School in California, improvisation is:

- provocative competence: deliberate efforts to interrupt habit patterns;

- embracing errors as a source of learning;

- orientation toward minimal structures that allow maximum flexibility;

- distributed task: continual negotiation and dialogue toward dynamic synchronization;

- reliance on retrospective sense-making;

- "hanging out": membership in a community of practice;

- taking turns soloing and supporting.[8]

Annie Pye notes that the character of improvising has much to offer leaders in the twenty-first century. Professor Annie Pye, from the school of management at Bath, England, and her colleague Ian Mangham, make clear that leadership shares with jazz improvisation such features as simultaneous reflection and action; simultaneous rule creation and rule following; patterns of mutually expected responses akin to musicians moving through a melody together; action informed by melodies in the form of codes; continuous mixing of the expected with the novel; and heavy reliance on intuitive grasp and imagination.[9]

Improvisation appears to be one of the appropriate models for the complex, volatile, and uncertain environment of today for the following reasons:

- small and incremental changes can be effected quickly, allowing fast responses to user requirements;

- improvisation provides high levels of feedback and closer contact between provider and client;

- design jamming is a collaborative effort with a learning audience and brings a provider/client relationship back into the equation;

- plans and routines are not the drivers, but the dynamic relationship with the customer is the main force for change;

- while improvisation won't handle all the challenges of training provision, it extends, the toolbox of strategies available to the practitioner;

- improvisation does not abandon more traditional models, but shapes, extends and enriches them.

The following description offered by Rosabeth Moss Kanter at the Harvard Business School, and quoted in a research article by Mary Crossan at the Richard Ivey School of Business, captures what improvisation means in a complex world:

To some companies, the context in which they are now entered seems increasingly less like baseball or other traditional games and more like the croquet game in *Alice in Wonderland* – a game that compels the player to deal with constant change. In that fictional game, nothing remains stable for very long, because everything is alive and changing around the player – an all-too-real condition for many managers. The mallet Alice uses is a flamingo, which tends to lift its head and face in another direction just as Alice tries to hit the ball. The ball, in turn, is a hedgehog, another creature with a mind of its own. Instead of lying there waiting for Alice to hit it, the hedgehog unrolls, gets up, moves to another part of the court, and sits down again. The wickets are card soldiers, ordered around by the Queen of Hearts, who changes the structure of the game seemingly at whim by barking out an order to the wickets to reposition themselves around the court.[10]

What improvisation fosters is an opportunity to design, act, learn, reflect, and renew. *Improvisation is a place where resourcefulness becomes more crucial than resources.*[11] Many leaders cite an assumed link between improvisation and innovation, and intentionally provide employees the organizational and temporal space to learn from experimentation and improvisation. Improvisation's spontaneous nature taxes the basic skills of listening and communicating. It demands that individuals give their full concentration and attention to the moment, rather than being preoccupied by what happened or what could happen. Improvisation also demonstrates that you need to be committed in order to be convincing. Leaders who are interested in implementing improvisation need to begin by developing their own capacity to improvise and cultivating their own capabilities to step in where required. The next step is to extend these skills to the team.

TRY THIS:

Rate Your Leadership Improvisation Capacities:

Have you built a fluid organization and team that is responsive to changing customer needs?

- Do you improvise when carrying out an action or do you always closely follow a plan?

TRY THIS:

Applying Improvisation in Everyday Life

Go on an empathy walk. Claus Otto Scharmer at MIT's Sloan School of Management suggests having conversations with individuals who are wholly different.[12] Examples could include having conversations with homeless persons; someone sitting next to you on the bus, train or subway; a person you have not previously engaged in dialogue at your next meeting, and so on. The goal is to learn to leave a safe territory and perceive what it means to engage with someone who has a different perspective. Leaders could also choose to step in the shoes of a front line team member.

There are additional tools to deal with complexity that tap into the nonconscious and enhance sense-making capability. What follows is an exploration of other movement tools, followed by several auditory or sound tools.

WHAT CAN SCULPTORS TEACH LEADERS?

Clay, like the brain has plasticity and is capable of continuous and permanent change of shape in any direction without breaking apart; it is moldable, pliable. The image of the potter's wheel and hand-building with clay, provides an excellent example of detachment in action, a way to be conscious in the midst of the nonconscious.

The first task for the potter is to centre all the elements and confine the clay on the rotating wheel. In order for this to take place, the mind has to be stilled. The hands do the work; if a thought enters, such as, "I am going to make a perfect pot," the process is ruined and the pot is knocked off centre. A steady detachment must be maintained: the action is performed but the doer does not claim the fruits. Sitting above the spinning wheel, distanced yet intimately involved, the witness silently watches the pot grow and take shape. There is reciprocity between the stillness – the authentic consciousness – and the activity, the realm of manifestation, the nonconscious pot, which is being created. The two modes work together for the creation of a new order.

This skill in action, taken beyond the metaphor of the potter's wheel, can liberate the leader to move through issues using what is needed but avoiding the pitfalls in inauthentic consciousness. When thinking fills up with ideas preoccupied with the sense of self, it becomes impossible to move unencumbered; when the thinking is pacified, it no longer inserts the artificial "I" barrier between the pure witness and the task at hand. Consciousness becomes authentic when "I," "me," or "mine" no longer intrudes. Self-conscious identity must be removed in order for the silent unseen witness to be realized.

According to Toby Rhodes, a senior lecturer in human resource management at Sheffield Hallam University, and Vivien Whitaker, a sculptor and lecturer, "sculpture is a kinesthetic activity that can stimulate deep and creative thinking and learning at individual, team and organizational levels. Sculpture engages participants on many levels: it is practical, creative, artistic, playful, and collaborative. For most people, creating meaningful sculpture is an unfamiliar task that offers the opportunity to work in the stretch zone. Sculpture projects empower learners to create something new and original – they give responsibility for the outcome and process to the learners."[13]

Creating improvised sculpture is a powerful group process because it embodies depth, application to real work issues, accessibility, and flexibility. Creating sculpture engages the nonconscious brain, using metaphor, symbolism and imagery.

TRY THIS:

Shaping and molding clay opens the door to a leader's own perception and needs. There is nothing at stake here; you can leave your conscious thoughts behind.

1. Make an icon from a ball of clay by slowly rolling and kneading the clay with your hands. Avoid premature closure and expand your perceptions in terms of what might be possible.

2. Close your eyes while working the clay. Concentrate on how the material feels. Notice what you notice.

3. Give your imagination free rein, and shape the sphere into a sculpture that represents you as a leader. It can be an abstract form or a real object. Something might emerge from a least expected source.

4. When you have finished your work of art, concentrate on how you feel, what the figure means to you and why you decided to make it. Does the figure connect to your leadership goals?

WHAT CAN THEATRE TEACH LEADERS?

Life is theatre; we are all actors every day and in every situation. William Gardner and Bruce Avolio suggest that leadership is a process enacted theatrically in acts of *framing, scripting, staging,* and *performing*.[14] Theatre is actually the staging of images and the staging of texts. What is leadership in that context, what is important? How can theatre techniques and methodologies assist leaders in making sense of complexity in today's world?

Using Shakespearean monologues, improvised short scenes, theatrical warmup, and coaching for final dramatic presentations, the Ariel Group, a Boston Massachusetts based consulting firm, provides opportunities for leaders to explore and improve their presence. Presence is being aware, accessing the nonconscious and listening with stillness. Christopher Von Bayer of the Ariel Group identifies four dimensions of presence necessary for leaders to be effective:

- be present: be centred and aware in each moment of communication;
- reach out: build and sustain authenticity with the audience;
- be expressive: communicate dynamically and congruently with voice, body, mind, and emotion;
- be self-knowing: reflect and leverage the one's own unique identity as a person and professional.[15]

The value of using theatre as a metaphor to develop leadership capability is particularly evident in the leader's authenticity and performance.

TRY THIS:

Try an improvisational exercise called "Switch" which demonstrates the challenges associated with shifting leadership.[16] Pick another person to begin to play out a scene. When an observer sees an opportunity to step in, they call "freeze" and replace the player by assuming their physical position. The new player restarts the action, taking the scene in an entirely new direction. Individuals must be alert to the opportunities in the situation and what they can offer to move the scene forward. When a new person enters, the person remaining must be ready to support the new direction.

TRY THIS:

In an exercise called "Make a Story" participants provide a title and the "players" improvise and build additional ideas on the story. The players take their turn at the "director's" cue.

Next we examine the sound tools, which will be referred to as "Sound Explorer" and include narrative or storytelling, listening, and music.

WHAT CAN NARRATIVE TEACH LEADERS?

Find stories, tell stories, and get others to tell stories. Make them up if necessary. Stories have created and sustained human tribes and communities for thousands of years. There's no greater example of the brain's powers of self-creation than the universal human practice of constructing narratives, of drawing from the raw stuff of experience the stories with which our brain explains itself to itself and to other brains. Mary Sue Seigel, a storyteller by profession, says, "Storytelling is central to every culture, and when you find that kind of universality, you know it's not just social learning but reflects something deep-seated in our genes... coherent stories are an integration of the drive to tell a logical story about events and the ability to grasp emotionally the mental processes of the people in those events."[17]

Storytelling relies on the prefrontal short- and long-term memory systems and the cerebellum, once thought to coordinate only physical movement, but now believed to coordinate different emotional and cognitive functions. Storytelling involves planning, sequencing ideas, using language coherently, shifting attention, and interacting appropriately with other people.

Why is storytelling so paramount? Stories link the factual to the emotional, the specific to the universal, and the past to the present. A child hearing a story thinks, "there are others like me." Storytelling provides a template for self-expression, logic, and setting priorities. In sharing stories, team members are connected at many levels of the mind, which translates to many levels of the brain. Storytelling is gaining recognition as a useful leadership tool that provides leaders with a richer insight into their own behaviour and attitudes. Stephen Denning, director of the World Bank's knowledge management program, suggests that more and more organizations now recognize that storytelling can:

- communicate complex new ideas and spark energetic action toward their implementation;

- be remarkably effective, even in the most adverse circumstances, both in the public and private sector;

- be mastered by a wide variety of individuals in a short period of time, because it draws on the latent capacity for storytelling that all human beings possess;

- be an informative and entertaining way to help leaders expose non-verbalized feelings as well as behaviours associated with product/service usage.[18]

Organizations and individuals construct and reconstruct meaning. The power of narrative is in its ability to provide leaders with an essential tool by which they can sense-make and sense-give: "Whether leading one person or thousands, cultivating narrative enables the leader to locate important themes, communicate those themes, and creatively live them out in daily life. Because the journey from ambiguity to opportunity is ongoing, leaders and organizations can grow competent in negotiating the cycle as they tap the power of narrative. In doing so, everyone learns to appreciate more fully the 'organizational adventure' that lies ahead."[19]

Stories are effective as learning tools because they are believable, memorable, and entertaining. The believability stems from the fact that stories deal with human or human-like experience that we tend to perceive as an authentic and credible source of knowledge. Stories make information more memorable because they involve us in the actions and intentions of the characters. Stories invite and demand active meaning making.

We must fill in, from our own store of knowledge, that which is unspoken. In so doing, we create as well as discover meaning, and we pose the questions we ourselves need to answer.

The leader-involvement factor is also related to the power of stories to stimulate empathic responses. It is the particularity of the story – the specific situation, the small details, and the vivid images of human experience – that evokes a fuller response than does a simple statement of fact. This fuller response provides the raw material for both cognitive appreciation and affective response to the experience of another person.[20] Leadership development that aims to foster tolerance, appreciation of diversity, and a capacity for perspective-taking can draw upon this dynamic of storytelling.

Stories educate as instruments of transformation as well as information. Because stories lead from the familiar to the unfamiliar, they provide an entryway to a possibility of personal growth and change. As Evelyn Clark, an organizational consultant notes, it is when one can identify with a character that has changed that one can envision and embrace the possibility of change for oneself.[21] Stories of achievement and transformation can function as motivators, pathfinders, and sources of encouragement. In short, stories enable us to engage with new knowledge, broaden perspectives, and expand possibilities because we encounter them in the familiar territory of human experience.

Just as stories are powerful voice tools, listening tools are also critical in developing leadership capability.

LISTEN WITH A THIRD EAR

Question: Why were leaders given two ears but only one mouth?

Answer: Because the creator knew that listening was twice as hard as talking.

Enhanced listening combined with storytelling and visualization are very powerful components in the leadership sense-making process.

A leader's failure to listen frequently results from hearing only what they want to hear and remembering only part of what they heard. Most of us spend between 70 to 80 percent of our waking lives communicating, and nearly half of that time (45 percent) is spent listening. But we are poor listeners; we listen at an efficiency rate of only between 25 to 50 percent. One reason for this may be that the average person speaks at a rate between 150 to 200 words per minute (WPM), but we can hear at a rate of at least 600 WPM. That leaves a lot of time for our minds to wander. Another reason is that when someone is talking, most of us are thinking about how we're going to respond. Many misunderstandings can be attributed to the expectation factor, that is, when the recipient (or listener) perceives that they heard what they expected to hear in the message transmitted. Leaders and team members alike tend to hear what they expect to hear.

The ability to listen involves turning on attention, recognizing flow, and watching with open minds and ears that which presents itself in the moment. Robert Haskell, a professor of psychology at the University of New England, believes another benefit to deep listening is that nonconscious feelings can be revealed by the words, metaphors, and topics that are used in conversations.[22]

WHAT CAN MUSIC TEACH LEADERS?

Figure 8-2: Leadership Metaphor?

Music may be one of the purest human languages that communicates to everyone. As in all works of art, music has the ability to express thoughts and emotions. Musical metaphors like the "jamming" of Jazz essentially mean playing with and not always by the rules, and creating new ones. We are all by nature musical rhythmic people. We are surrounded by music every day, and enjoy it for relaxation, and may even dance to it. Music can also enhance our thinking ability.

Research published in the February 1997 issue of <u>Neurological Research</u> suggests that listening to music can enhance spatial reasoning performance.[23] The studies of Frances Rauscher, a research psychologist, and neuro scientist Gordon Shaw, Ph.D., representing a research team from the University of California at Irvine confirm an unmistakable causal link between music and spatial intelligence. They note, "Well-developed spatial intelligence is the ability to perceive the visual world accurately, to form mental images of physical objects, and to recognize variations of objects."[24] The researchers theorize that spatial reasoning abilities are crucial for such higher brain functions as music, complex mathematics, and chess. As many of the problems in which scientists and engineers engage in cannot be described in verbal form, progress in science may, in fact, be closely linked to the development of certain spatial skills."[25]

Kevin Asbjörnson, in his program called Artistry of Leadership, uses music as a tool for exploring leadership as art by combining piano music, journaling, reflection, imagination, and facilitated discussion. The purpose is to assist leaders in enhancing "connections, communications and meaning in the workplace."[26]

As part of his practice, Asbjörnson instructs groups to listen to a three-minute piano composition. As the piano plays, the participants write down the most significant theme, image, or pattern that appears to them. When the music has ended, each person shares their experience, which is then linked back to everyday leadership challenges. Again, the leader accesses the nonconscious brain: to explore issues of communication, mindfulness, and perspective as they relate to their leadership roles.

When listening to music with such close attention, leaders become fully present and begin to access the nonconscious brain. Being present is the key to being a good listener and to executing anything effectively. Yet, how many leaders practise this skill of being present? Using the kind of focus that allows for perception of classical music's nuances plants the seed of presence in the leader's relationship with others – co-workers, clients, suppliers, vendors, and other stakeholder groups.[27]

In summary, the study of music offers leaders a wealth of "tools" that can have a profound effect on their performance. Keen awareness, and rhythm and flow all work in concert to enhance our capacities and output.

HEARING AND EXPRESSING THE INNER VOICE OF THE LEADER

In this chapter movement, and sound (technologies for leveraging the nonconscious mind) were explored. Remember, 95 percent or more of all thought occurs in the nonconscious, nonaware mind, and yet most people miss this hidden inner voice. Hearing and expressing this inner voice is important since it predicts actual behaviour better than consciously expressed thoughts and feelings, and potentially leads to more effective decision-making and problem-solving.

AFTERWORD

Today's world appears to be captured in the following statement: If we know anything for sure, it is only that no one knows anything for sure. More and more organizations are realizing that *stability and predictability are no longer reasonable assumptions.* In fact, the number one challenge of today's leader's is getting their organizations and teams to adapt to an environment that is neither stable nor predictable. How do we make sense and meaning of what's happening in this climate of uncertainty and volatility? How does a leader stay a leader during tumultuous times?

The leader's natural response is to analyze challenges and issues, assess risk, and then quickly seek a solution. This can work quite well when it comes to routine issues, but in cases where complexity and uncertainty dominate it may be more important to suspend action, look, listen, and then to attempt some act which flows harmoniously out of the whole meaning, movement, and essence of the situation.

Logical analysis and blueprints do not naturally move us toward nor assist us in navigating this uncharted world. On the contrary, the logical brain was always designed to serve as a guide for the imagination. It was never intended to function on its own.

Instead, leaders need to have imaginative powers that are sensitive enough to pick out what's moving out of the corner of the eye.

> I have learned to trust my peripheral mind and to bring quick or fleeting perceptions more sharply into focus. If I sit in a chair and try concertedly to come up with a good idea, nothing very exciting will happen. I think it's important to have an awareness of the territory which interests you, but to avoid the potential constraints inherent in this kind of focus.[1]

The new leader needs to be not only a decision-maker who can think strategically, but also a sense-maker who creates context, recognizes patterns, and can sense that which cannot yet be seen. As John Seely Brown says "The challenge in the old economy is to make product. The challenge in the digital economy is to make sense."[2] It is a journey that needs to be taken with a candle rather than a flashlight, a blank canvas rather than a blueprint, using the urgings of a nonconscious and imaginative mind as the guide. By setting aside our mindsets we create the ground for new perspectives and insights to emerge. In this spirit of openness and curiosity we begin to find the solutions.

As a consequence, the role of the leader is shaped less by that which is "known" and can be "controlled" and more by how perception is shaped, seeing with fresh eyes, learning from actions, and reshaping knowledge based on new experiences, perspectives, and ideas. Inherent in this change is the leader's ability to access the nonconscious brain and use the tools that assist in that process. Art as a metaphor skillfully uses leadership that ultimately makes sense of complexity and uncertainty, finding connections between images emerging from the nonconscious – making the invisible visible.

Essentially, leadership is all about balancing the logical conscious brain with learning to listen to the nonconscious and being able to cultivate a relaxed mind. Very innovative people may be able to do this intuitively, and it is important to realize that we are all born with innovative minds.

APPENDIX:
USING ART IN DEVELOPING LEADERSHIP[1]

A not-for-profit organization (NPO) uses a mixture of photographs and collage to create active participation during an offsite strategic retreat. Scenes depicting organizational strategy are also visually displayed to capture suggestions for innovation. Participants engage in debate and differences of view surface. Consensus is reached and new strategic areas are identified.

A financial services organization uses drama and improvisation to explore team differences and values. Participants develop and act out scenes reflecting personal attitudes and values in the organization. Areas of differences surface and a plan is identified to build an effective team.

A utilities organization creates a vision statement through the use of sculpture. Using clay materials, sculptures are created which result in ideas for leveraging efficiencies in the organization. Individual sculptures created by managers are explored and discussed and result in debate and dialogue. The sculptures are formed into a gallery and provide a backdrop for the rest of the session. They portray strategic intent in a way that words are unable to.

A public sector organization uses drama and working with scripts to identify areas for process improvement and efficiencies. They work with masks representing varied financial approaches. Wearing and creating different masks assists the team to identifying strengths and weaknesses in fiscal approaches.

For additional information and tools using the H-SAT (Heemsbergen Sensory Awareness Tools), please contact the author at, bastiaan@sympatico.ca or www.drbastiaan.com.

ENDNOTES

INTRODUCTION ENDNOTES

1. Ronald Kotulak, I*nside the Brain, Revolutionary Discoveries of How the Mind Works* (Kansas City: Andrews and McMeel, A Universal Press Syndicate Company, 1996), 6-7,155-167.

2. Antonio R. Damasio, Descartes' *Error: Emotion, Reason, and the Human Brain* (New York: Avon Books, 1994), 259.

3. Melissa Szalkowski, "Brain Repair Yourself", in "Better Brains, How Neuroscience will Enhance You," Scientific American, Sept. 2003, 47.

4. Ibid.

5. Ibid.

6. Daniel Drubach, *The Brain Explained* (Upper Saddle River, New Jersey: Prentice-Hall, 2000).

7. M. Proust, *Remembrance of Things Past (A la recherche du temps perdu), Vol. 1* (New York: Vintage, 1981).

8. Karl E. Weick, *Making Sense of the Organization Managing the Unexpected: Assuring High Performance in an Age of Complexity* (San Franciso: Jossey-Bass, 2001).

9. Robert Simon, "Eye Believe, or I Believe: The Relationship of Perception to Reality," 17 July, 2002, <http://www.kmuw.org/stories/simon/2002/believe.html>.

10. Ibid.

11. Behavioral Finance Characteristics Explained, Rutgers Cooperative Extension, <http://www.rce.rutgers.edu/money2000/pressroom/release.asp?id=107>.

12. G. Lakoff, and M. Johnson, *Philosophy in the Flesh: the Embodied Mind and Its Challenge to Western Though*, 1st ed. (New York: Basic Books, 1999), 10.

CHAPTER ONE ENDNOTES

1. European Dana Alliance for the Brain, "Achievements and Challenges of the Decade of the Brain," EuroBrain 2, 1 March 2000, <http://www.edab.net/>.

2. "The Hows, Whats and Whos of Neuroscience," <http://faculty.washington.edu/chudler/introb.html>.

3. Jerome R. Gardner, "Cognitive Behavior Management Practice." <http://www.cognitivebehavior.com/practice/concepts/practice.html>.

4. Melissa Szalkowski, "Brain Repair Yourself," in "Better Brains, How Neuroscience will Enhance You," *Scientific American*, Sept. 2003, 467.

5. B. Pakkenberg, et.al. "Aging and the Human Neocortex," *Exp.Gerontology* 38 2003: 95-99; B. Pakkenberg and H.J.G. Gundersen, "Neocortcial Neuron Number in Humans: Effect of Sex and Age." J. Comp. Neurology 384 1997: 312-320. B. Pakkenberg et al., 1997.

6. Ronald Kotulak, *Inside the Brain-Revolutionary Discoveries of How the Mind Works* (Kansas City: Andrews and McMeel, A Universal Press Syndicate Company, 1996), 144.

7. Ibid.

8. Society for Neuroscience, "Brain Facts: A Primer on the Brain and Nervous System," 4th ed. (Washington, DC: Society for Neuroscience, 2002).

9. Ibid.

10. Ibid.

11. Ibid.

12. Ibid.

13. Kotulak, 144.

14. Robert Goffee, and Gareth Jone, "Why Should Anyone Be Led by You?" *Harvard Business Review* (Sept. 2000).

15. Ronald Kotulak, 13.

16. Douglas S. Fox, "The Inner Savant," *Discover 23*, no. 2 February 2002.

17. Lawrence Osborne, "*Savant For a Day*: Transcranial Magnetic Stimulation," New York Times, section 6, 38 Column 1, 27 June, 2003.

18. Fox, 2002, 3.

19. Osborne, 38.

20. Ibid.

21. BBC 1, "Fragments of Genius." 10 March 2001, <http://news.bbc.co.uk/1/hi/health/1211299.stm>.

22. Darold Treffert, "Extraordinary People: Understanding Savant Syndrome Investigation of Latent Savant Skills Using Transcranial Magnetic Stimulation," 2000, <http://www.wisconsinmedicalsociety.org/savant/rtms.cfm>.

23. Ibid.

24. Allan Snyder and Mandy Thomas, "Autistic Artists Give Clues to Cognition," Centre for the Mind, Australian National University, 2002, <http://www.centreforthemind.com/publications/ Autistic_artists.cfm>.

25. Ibid.

26. Alan Snyder, "The Mind's New Science," Keynote address presented at Cognitive Science Miniconference, Macquarie University, November 1996, <http://www.centreforthemind.com/publications/ Breaking_Mindset.cfm>.

27. L. Selfe, Nadia; *A Case of Extraordinary Drawing Ability in an Autistic Child* (London: Academic Press, 1977).

28. Bruce Miller, "A passion for painting (Vital Signs)" *Discover*, 23 No. 2, (Jan.1998).

29. John Mitchell, and Allan Snyder, "How Do They Do It? – Savants," Proceedings of the Royal Society Biological Sciences, vol. 266, no.1419, (1999): 537-647.

30. Ibid.

31. Ibid.

32. Ibid.

33. Ibid.

34. Ibid.

35. Allan Snyder, 'Genius, Madness and Innovation" (paper presented The Australian Academy of Technological Sciences and Engineering Owning Innovation – From Idea to Delivery Academy Symposium, November 2002), <http://www.atse.org.au/publications/symposia/proc-2002p1.htm>.

36. Snyder and Mitchell, "Is Integer Arithmetic Fundamental to Mental Processing? The Mind's Secret Arithmetic", 587-592.

37. Bruce Miller, *Geniuses, Prodigies & Savants Extraordinary People – What Makes Them Tick?* Australian National University & University of Sydney: Centre for the Mind, Joint Venture, 2002, <http://www.centreforthemind.com>.

38. Ibid.

39. Bruce Miller et al., "Emergence of Artistic Talent in Frontotemporal Dementia," *Neurology* 51 (1998): 978-82.

40. Ibid.

41. Mitchell and Snyder, "How Do They Do It? – Savants," 50 - 51

42. Darold Treffert, "Extraordinary People: Understanding Savant Syndrome," (2000), <http://www.wisconsinmedicalsociety.org/savant/rtms.cfm>

43. Fox, 2002, 4.

CHAPTER TWO ENDNOTES

1. Antonio R. Damasio, *Descartes' Error: Emotion, Reason, and the Human Brain* (New York: Avon Books 1994), 259.

2. Emmanuel Ransford Panpsychism, "The Conscious Brain and Exo-Biological Awareness," Proceedings of Association of Nigerian Physicians in America 19, Cambridge, (September 1998).

3. George A. Miller, "The Magical Number Seven – Plus or Minus Two: Some Limits on our Capacity for Processing Information," *The Psychological Review*, 63, 2 (March 1956).

4. Benjamin Libet et al., "Subjective Referral of the Timing for a Conscious Sensory Experience," *Brain* 102 (1979): 193-224.

5. Gerald Zaltman, *How Customers Think: Essential Insights into the Mind of the Market* (Cambridge, MA: Harvard Business School Press, 2003).

6. Ibid.

7. Ibid.

8. Ibid.

9. Mark S. George, "Stimulating The Brain," *Scientific American*, Sept. 2003 34.

10. Ibid.

11. T.L. Morrell, R.L. Young, and M.C. Ridding, "Investigation of Latent Savant Skills Using Transcranial Magnetic Stimulation," (honours thesis, University of South Australia, 2000).

12. Ibid.

13. Peter M. Senge et. al., *The Dance of Change: The Challenges to Sustaining Momentum in Learning* (New York: Currency Doubleday, 1999).

CHAPTER 3 ENDNOTES

1. Eric W. Weisstein, "Rabbit-Duck Illusion," *MathWorld*, A Wolfram Web Resource, <http://mathworld.wolfram.com/Rabbit-DuckIllusion.htm>l.

2. Donald Hoffman, *Visual Intelligence How We Create What We See* (New York: W. W. Norton & Company, Inc. 1999).

3. E.B. Goldstein, *Sensation and perception 6th ed.* (Pacific Grove, CA: Wadsworth, 2002).

4. Ibid.

5. Ellen Langer, *Mindfulness* (Reading, MA: Addison-Wesley, 1989).

6. Robert C. Priddy, "The Human Whole, An Outline Of Higher Psychology," 1999, <http://home.no.net/rrpriddy/psy/>.

7. Ibid.

8. Dexter Dunphy, *"In search of the future,"*
   Keynote address to the 4th Annual Conference on Spirituality,
   Leadership, and Management Rydges Resort, Eaglehawk Hill,
   Canberra Australia, Dec. 2001), 5.

9. M.J. Wheatley, *Leadership and the New Science*
   (San Francisco, CA: Berrett-Koehler, 1992).

10. B. L. Miller, et al., "Emergence of Artistic Talent in
    Frontotemporal Dementia," *Neurology* 51 (1998): 978-982.

11. A.G. Greenwald and M.R. Banaji, "Implicit Social Cognition:
    Attitudes, Self-esteem, and Stereotypes," *Psychological Review*
    102, 1 (1995): 4-27.

12. Daniel L. Simons and M.T. Levine, "Change blindness," *Trends
    in Cognitive sciences* 1, 2 (1997): 261-267.

13. Laura Spinney, "How Much of the World Do We Really See?"
    New Scientist, 27 Nov. 2000.

14. "Epsych Web Page," Mississippi State University, "The
    Deliberate Mind," <http://www.epsych.msstate.edu/>.

15. Gary Hamel, "Strategy Innovation and the Quest for Value,"
    Sloan Management Review 39, no. 2, (Winter 1998): 78-85.

16. Hamel, 83.

17. Gary Hamel, "E -Corp: Inside the revolution, Avoiding the
    Guillotine," *Fortune*, April 2, 2001.

18. Thomas Kuhn, *The Structure of Scientific Revolutions* 3rd ed.
    (Chicago: University Press, 1996).

19. Karl Weick, "Drop Your Tools: An Allegory for Organizational
    Studies," *Administrative Science Quarterly* 41 (1996): 301-313.

20. Joseph Jaworski and Claus Otto Scharmer, "The New Economy: Sensing and Actualizing Emerging Futures" Society for Organizational Learning (Cambridge and Beverly, Mass.: Generon Consulting, 2000).

21. Abraham Kaplan, *The Conduct of Inquiry: Methodology for Behavioral Science* (Scranton, PA: Chandler, 1964): 3.

22. Ibid.

23. K. Duncker, "On Problem Solving" trans. L. S. Lees, *Psychological Monographs* 58, no. 270 (1945).

24. Langer, 1989, 152.

25. Marlene C. Fiol, C. and Edward J. O'Connor, "Waking Up! Mindfulness in the Face of Bandwagons," *Academy of Management Review* 28 no.1 (2003): 59.

26. Thomas Davenport, and John. C. Beck, *The Attention Economy*, (Cambridge: Harvard Business School Press, 2001).

27. Ibid.

CHAPTER FOUR ENDNOTES

1. C. Alexander and E. Langer, eds., *Higher Stages of Human Development* (New York: Oxford University, 1990).

2. Ibid.

3. Ellen Langer, "Minding Matters: The Consequences of Mindlessness," in L. Berkowitz (ed.), *Advances in Experimental Social Psychology* (San Diego: Academic Press, 1998), 138.

4. William Luckert and Alec Horniman, "Why Must a Leader be a Learner," "Leader Learning" (Fall 2001), <http://www.linezine.com/6.2/articles/wlahwmlbl.html>.

5. Jack Demick, "Toward a Mindful Psychological Science: Theory and Application," *Journal of Social Issues* 56 (Spring 2001): 16.

6. Ellen J. Langer, and Mihnea Moldoveanu, "The Construct of Mindfulness," *Journal of Social Issues* 56 (Spring 2000): 1-9.

7. Ellen J. Langer, *Mindfulness* (Reading, MA: Addison Wesley. 1989): 167.

8. Ibid. 4.

9. Eileen K. McCluskey, "When 1 and 1 Are Not 2," *Harvard University Gazette*, (16 January 1997), <http://www.news.harvard.edu/gazette/1997/01.16/>.

10. Steven C. Hayes, "Mindfulness: Method and Process," *Clinical Psychology: Science and Practice* 10 no. 2, (May 2003): 161-165.

11. Toni Searle, "UCITE speaker addresses mindfulness," <http://www.cwru.edu/pubaff/univcomm/rel-archive/langer.htm>.

12. Eileen McCluskey.

13. Jack Demick, 16.

14. Ellen J. Langer, *The Power of Mindful Learning* (Reading, MA: Addison-Wesley, 1997).

15. Marlene C. Fiol and Edward J. O'Connor, "Waking Up! Mindfulness in the Face of Bandwagons," *Academy of Management Review* 28 no.1, (2003): 59.

16. Ellen J. Langer, "Mindful Learning," *Current Directions in Psychological Science* 9 no.6, (2000): 38 – 41.

17. Langer and Moldoveanu, 1–9.

18. Ellen Langer, Kurt Masur and Sarah Chang Interview, *Lincoln Center for the Performing Arts*, New York, March 3, 1998, <http://www.pbs.org/lflc/backstage/march3/langer.htm>.

19. A.T. Beck, *Cognitive Therapy and the Emotional Disorders* (New York: International Universities Press, 1976).

CHAPTER FIVE ENDNOTES

1. Ellen J. Langer, *The Power of Mindful Learning* (New York: Addison-Wesley, 1997).

2. E. Jones, *Sigmund Freud, Life and Work*, 2 vols. (London: Hogarth Press, 1955).

3. Ron Ruggles, "The State of the Notion – Knowledge Management in Practice," *California Management Review* 40, no. 3 (September, 1998): 80-90.

4. Ibid.

5. Daniel Pink, "Metaphor Marketing," *Fast Company*, no. 14 (April 1998): 214.

6. Harald Atmanspacher, "Mind and Matter as Asymptotically Disjoint, Inequivalent representations with Broken Time-reversal symmetry," *BioSystems* 68 (2003): 19-30.

7. Alain J. Gauthier, "An Integral Approach to Executive Leadership Development," 2002, <http://www.coreleadership.com/exdev.html>.

8. John Seely Brown and Paul Duguid, *The Social Life of Information* (Boston: Harvard Business School Press, 2000).

9. Allan W. Snyder, "Breaking Mindset," *Mind and Language* 13, (1997): 1-10.

10. James Hillman, *Egalitarian Typologies Versus the Perception of the Unique* (Dallas: Spring Publications, 1980).

11. Joseph Jaworski, Claus Otto Scharmer et al., "Leadership in the Context of Emerging Worlds: Illuminating the Blind Spot," Summary Paper on an Ongoing Research Project, 20 Propositions Based on Conversations Among the Authors and Dialogue Interviews with Thought Leaders on Knowledge and Leadership, McKinsey–Society for Organizational Learning (SOL) Leadership Project (1999-2000).

12. Ibid.

13. Ibid.

14. Ibid.

15. Semir Seki, *Inner Vision: An Exploration of Art and the Brain* (New York: Oxford University Press, 1990).

16. Ibid.

17. Ibid.

18. Joseph Goguen, Nicholas Humphrey, and Eric Harth, "Art and the Brain: Controversies in Science and the Humanities," *Journal of Consciousness Studies* 6 (June - July 1999).

19. David Kelley, *The Art of Innovation: Lessons in Creativity from Ideo, America's Leading Design Firm* (New York: Doubleday, 2001).

20. H.O. Mounce, *Tolstoy on Aesthetics - What Is Art?* (Hampshire, UK: Ashgate Publishing, 2002).

21. Peter Drucker, *Management: Tasks, Responsibilities, Practices* (New York, Harper Business, 1993), 485.

22. Curtis Sittenfeld, "The Creative Odyssey How Idea Companies Get Their Ideas," *Fast Company*, no. 8 (October 1999): 54.

23. Ibid.

24. Ibid.

25. John Dewey, *Art as Experience* (Penguin Putnam, 1934).

26. Ibid.

27. Ibid.

28. Tom Zeit, "How to Develop the Eye of an Artist," *Artist's Sketchbook* (July 2003).

29. Claus Otto Scharmer, "Presencing – A Social Technology of Freedom," *Trigon Themen* (Feb. 2002).

30. Ibid.

31. Chuck Palus and David Horth, *The Leader's Edge: Six Creative Competencies for Navigating Complex Challenges* (San Francisco: Jossey - Bass, 2002).

32. Ibid.

33. Tony Buzan and Raymond Keene, *Book of Genius and How to Unleash Your Own* (New York: Random House, 1994).

34. Ibid.

35. Michael J. Gelb, *How to Think Like Leonardo da Vinci: Seven Steps to Genius Every Day* (New York: Random House 1998).

CHAPTER 6 ENDNOTES

1. Lillian Hellman, *Pentimento: A Book of Portraits* (New York: Back Bay Books, 2000).

2. Claus Otto Scharmer, "Self-Transcending Knowledge: Organizing Around Emerging Realities." in *Managing Industrial Knowledge: Creation, Transfer and Utilization*, Ikujiro Nonaka and David J. Teece, eds. (London: Sage, 2001), 87.

3. B. Pakkenberg, et.al., "Aging and the Human Neocortex,"
Exp. Gerontology 38 (2003): 95 - 99, B. Pakkenberg, and
H.J.G.Gundersen, "Neocortical Neuron Number in Humans:
Effect of Sex and Age," *J. Comp. Neurology* 384 (1997):
312 - 320.

4. Society for Neuroscience, "Brain Facts: A Primer on the Brain
and Nervous System," *The Society for Neuroscience* 6, no. 2 (2002).

5. Ralph Stacey, *Strategic Management and Organizational
Dynamics*, 4th ed. (New York: Prentice Hall, 2002).

6. Mihaly Csikszentmihalyi, *Creativity* (New York: HarperCollins,
1996).

7. Christina Cavanagh, *Managing Your E-Mail: Thinking Outside
the Inbox*, (Mississauga: John Wiley & Sons Canada, 2003).

8. Daniel Goleman, Emotional intelligence: *Why It Can Matter
More Than IQ* (New York: Bantam Books, 1995).

9. Michael Andreas Gielen "Right Brain Workouts – Foreigners,"
<http://www.gocreate.com/Workouts/wx095.htm>.

10. Colin Funk, interview by author, Banff Centre, Banff, Alberta,
Canada, April 2002.

11. Curtis Sittenfield, "The Most Creative Man in Silicon Valley,"
Fast Company, no. 35 (June 2000): 274.

12. F. Varela, "Neurophenomenology: A Methodological Remedy to
the Hard Problem," J. *Consc. Studies* 3 (1996): 330-350. J.Shear
(Ed.), "Explaining Consciousness: The Hard Problem of
Consciousness," (Cambridge: MIT Press, 1997): 337-358

13. Rudyard Kipling, *Just So Stories* (New York: Doubleday, 1912).

14. Fred Smith, "Talking about Creativity,"
<http://www.nciia.net/resource_folder/entreguides/gettingstarted
/ideas1.html>.

15. Miriam-Rose Ungunmerr-Baumann, "Aboriginal Culture," *Compass Theology Review* no.1-2 (1988): 9-11

16. Mihaly Csikszentmihalyi, *Finding Flow: The Psychology of Engagement with Everyday Life* (New York: Basic Books,1997).

17. John Kao, *Jamming: The Art and Discipline of Business Creativity* (New York: Harper Collins, 1996).

18. Claus Otto Scharmer, "Self-Transcending Knowledge: Sensing and Organizing Around Emerging Opportunities," *Journal of Knowledge Management* 5, no. 2, (2001): 137-150.

19. Society for Neuroscience, "Brain Facts: A Primer on the Brain and Nervous system," *The Society for Neuroscience* 6, no. 2, (Winter 2003).

20. Ibid.

21. Ibid.

22. Ibid.

23. Ibid.

24. Ibid.

25. Ibid.

26. Ibid.

27. Paul Israel, *Edison: A Life of Invention* (New York: Wiley, 1998), viii, 552.

28. Arthur Conan Doyle, The Casebook of Sherlock Holmes, "The Adventures of the Blanched Soldier," <http://www.geocities.com/fa1931/british/conandoy/ blanched.html>.

29. Tor Norretranders, *The User Illusion: Cutting Consciousness Down to Size* (New York: Penguin Books 1998): 125.

30. Karl Weick, *Sensemaking in Organizations, Foundations for Organizational Science* (Sage Publications Inc. 1995).

31. Peter Lane, Jane Salk, and Marjorie Lyles, "Absorptive Capacity, Learning and Performance in International Joint Ventures," *Strategic Management Journal* 22 (2001): 1139-1161.

32. Brian W. Arthur, "Coming from Your Inner Self," Dialogue on Leadership Conversation with Xerox Parc, Palo Alto, California, 16 April 1999, <http://www.dialogonleadership.org/Arthur-1999.html>.

33. Pete Wilkie, "Situational Awareness Lucky or Good?" *Flying Safety*, October 2001, 89.

34. Ibid.

35. B. McGuinness and L. Foy, A subjective measure of SA: The Crew Awareness Rating Scale. In D. B. Kaber and M. R. Endsley (Eds). *Human performance, situation awareness and automation: User centered design for the new millennium* (Atlanta: SA Technologies, 2000).

36. Ibid.

37. Al Andrade, *Harvard Project Zero*, The Thinking Classroom Cognitive Skills Group, Harvard Project Zero, 1999, <http://www.learnweb.harvard.edu/alps/thinking/reflect activities.cfm>.

38. Ibid.

39. John Kao, and Claus Scharmer, "The Seventh Career: Building an Innovation Keiretsu." John Kao, conversation with author, the Idea Factory, San Francisco 12 April, 2000. The conversation with John Kao took place as part of a global interview project involving twenty five interviews with eminent thinkers on knowledge and leadership (sponsored by McKinsey & Company and the Society for Organizational Learning). The interviews and the summary paper are accessible as free downloads from, <http://www.dialogonleadership.org>.

40. Mihaly Csikszentmihalyi and Eugene Rochberg-Halton, *The Meaning of Things: Domestic Symbols and the Self* (Cambridge: Cambridge University Press, 1981).

41. Janetta Mitchell McCoy and Gary W. Evans, "The Potential Role of the Physical Environment in Fostering Creativity," *Creativity Research Journal* 14 (October 2002): 409-426.

CHAPTER SEVEN ENDNOTES

1. Thia von Ghyczy, "The Fruitful Flaws of Strategy Metaphors," *Harvard Business Review* (September 2003): 86-94.

2. Ibid.

3. Ibid.

4. Lotte Darsa, "Arts in business - Proposing a Theoretical Framework," (paper presented at the European Academy of Management (EURAM) second annual conference on Innovative Research in Management, Stockholm, Sweden September 2002), <http://www.lld.dk/consortia/thecreativealliance/projects/ artsinbusiness/files/artsinbusiness/en/file view>.

5. Gareth Morgan, *Imaginization: New Mindsets for Seeing, Organizing and Managing* (Newbury Park and San Francisco: Sage Publications, 1993).

6. Ibid.

7. J. E. LeDoux, *The Emotional Brain* (New York: Simon & Schuster 1996).

8. Susanne K. Langer, *Mind, An Essay on Human Feeling* (Baltimore: The Johns Hopkins University Press,1967).

9. D. Laird, *Approaches to Training and Development*. (Reading, Mass.: Addison-Wesley, 1985).

10. Ibid.

11. Banff Centre Press release, "Quintessence, A Summit on the Science and Art of Visualization," (25 August 2002).

12. Clayton Nicholas, "The Emergence of Data Visualization Prospects for Its Business Applications," *Dr. John Meinke* Masters of Information Systems Management Professional Seminar, University of Maryland System Bowie State University, Heidelberg, Germany, August 1999, <http://faculty.ed.umuc.edu/~meinkej/inss690/nicholas/ INSS%20690-Data%20Visualization%20Paper.htmIbid>.

13. Ibid.

14. Yasin Rutrel, "CA To Deliver Next - Generation E-Commerce Platform," *Internet Week.com* 14 June 1999, <http://www.internetweek.com/story/showArticle.jhtml? articleID=640462>.

15. Nancy Margulies and Nusa Maal, *Mapping Inner Space* (Tucson, Ariz.: Zephyr Press, 2001).

16. Ibid.

17. Chuck Frey, "Visualize Your Goals," (7 Sept. 2001). <http://www.innovationtools.com/Articles/SuccessDetails. asp?a=11>.

18. Ibid.

19. John Kao, and Claus Otto Scharmer, "The Seventh Career: Building an Innovation Keiretsu." John Kao, conversation with author, the Idea Factory, San Francisco 12 April, 2000. The conversation with John Kao took place as part of a global interview project involving twenty five interviews with eminent thinkers on knowledge and leadership (sponsored by McKinsey & Company and the Society for Organizational Learning). The interviews and the summary paper are accessible as free downloads from, <http://www.dialogonleadership.org>.

20. Julia Cameron, "Leap and the net will appear," (February, 2003), <http://www.don-iannone.com/edfutures/2003_-1_26_ed-futures_archive.html>.

21. About Learning, "Visual Explorer: Educator's Edition Image Previews," <http://www.aboutlearning.com/visual_explorer/>.

22. Charles J. Palus and David M. Horth, *Visual Explorer: Picturing Approaches to Complex Challenges* (CCL Press, Greensboro, N.C.: 2001).

23. Ibid.

24. Carl E. Stafstrom, Kevin Rostasy, and Anna Minster, "The Usefulness of Children's Drawings in the Diagnosis of Headaches," *Pediatrics*, 109 (2002):460-472.

25. Nate Burgos, "Communicating Meaning: Drawing in Leadership," *LineZine Leader Learning*, (Fall 2001). <http://www.linezine.com/6.2/articles/nbcmdil.htm>.

26. Ibid.

27. Ibid.

28. Ibid.

29. Ibid.

30. Betty Edwards, *Drawing on the Right Side of the Brain* (New York: Tarcher/Putnam, 1989).

31. Eric Plotnick, "Concept Mapping: A Graphical System for Understanding the Relationship Between Concepts," ERIC Clearinghouse on Information and Technology, Syracuse NY. ERIC Digest, ERIC Identifier: ED407938, 1997.

32. Ibid.

33. Ibid.

34. Tony Buzan and Barry Buzan, *The Mind Map Book: How to Use Radiant Thinking to Maximize Your Brain's Untapped Potential* (London: BBC Consumer Publishing (Books), 1993).

35. Gabriele Lusser Rico, *Writing the Natural Way: Using Right-Brain Techniques to Release Your Expressive Powers* (New York: Penguin Putnam Inc., 2000).

36. Martha Lagace, "The Mind of the Market: Extending the Frontiers of Marketing Thought," HBS Working Knowledge, Harvard Business School (22 February 2000), <http://hbswk.hbs.edu/item.jhtml?id=1318&t=marketing>.

CHAPTER EIGHT ENDNOTES

1. John Kao, "The Art and Discipline of Business Creativity," *Strategy & Leadership* 25 (1997): 6-11

2. Stephen Leybourne, "The Project Management of Change within UK Financial Services: What About Improvisation?" paper presented at PMI Research Conference Seattle,WA., (14-17 July 2002), <http://www.newintermediaries.co.uk/archive/Leybourne PMI%202002.doc.>.

3. Ibid.

4. Karl Weick and F. Westley, "Organizational learning: Affirming an oxymoron," in S. R. Clegg, C. Hardy, and W. R. Nord (Eds.) *Handbook of Organization Studies*, (Thousand Oaks, CA: Sage, 1996), 453.

5. Karl Weick, "Organizational Redesign as Improvisation," in G.P. Huber, and W.H. (eds.), *Organizational Change and Redesign: Ideas and Insights for Improving Performance* (Oxford: Oxford University Press, 1993), 346-379.

6. Ibid.

7. Malcolm Webber, Michael Morgan, and Robert Dickson, "The Effect of Improvisation on Decision – Making in a Volatile Environment," *Journal of Organizational Leadership* 1, no. 1 (1999): 46-59.

8. F.J. Barrett, "Coda: Creativity and Improvisation in Organizations: Implications for Organizational Learning," *Organization Science* 9 (1998): 605-622.

9. Ian Mangham and Annie Pye, *The Doing of Managing* (Oxford: Blackwell, 1991), 18, 24, 40, 45, 78, 79.

10. M. Crossan, "Improvise to Innovate," *Business Quarterly* 62 no. 1 (1997): 36-42, M.M. Crossan, et al., "The Improvising Organization: Where Planning Meets Opportunity," *Organizational Dynamics* 24 no. 2 (1995): 20-35.

11. P.Z. Jackson, "Improvising in Training: Freedom Within Corporate Structures," *Journal of European Industrial Training* 19, 4 (1995): 25-28.

12. Claus Otto Scharmer and Kathrin Käufer, "Universities As the Birthplace for the Entrepreneurial Human Being," *Society for Organizational Learning* (August 2000): 8.

13. Toby Rhodes and Vivien Whitaker, "Creating Sculpture - Stimulating Learning," <http://www.ashridge.org.uk/web/leadconf2002.nsf/pages/journey>.

14. William L. Gardner, and Bruce J. Avolio, "The Charismatic Relationship: A Dramaturgical Perspective," *Management Review* 6, no. 2, (winter 2003): 32-58.

15. Kathy Halpern and Belle Lubar, *Leadership Presence Dramatic Techniques to Reach Out, Motivate, and Inspire* (New York: Penguin, 2003).

16. Colin Funk, interview by author, The Banff Centre, Banff, Alberta, Canada, November 2003.

17. Mary Sue Siegel, <http://www.geocities.com/marysuesiegel/ placesforstorytelling.html>.

18. Stephen Denning, The Springboard: *How Storytelling Ignites Action in Knowledge-Era Organizations* (Oxford: Elsevier Butterworth Heinemann, 2000).

19. David Fleming, "Narrative leadership: Using the Power of Stories" *Strategy & Leadership* 29, no. 4 (2001): 3.

20. Marsha Rossiter, "Narrative and Stories in Adult Teaching and Learning," ERIC Digest, P.1 ERIC Identifier: ED473147 (2002).

21. Evelyn Clarke, "Corporate Storytelling™ Fires Up Employees – and the Bottom Line," <http://www.corpstory.com/articles/personalleadership.htm\>.

22. Robert Haskell, *Deep Listening: Hidden Meanings in Everyday Conversations,* (Cambridge: Perseus Publishing 2001).

23. Gordon Shaw, Frances Rauscher, and Linda Levine, "Music and Spatial Task Performance - A Causal Relationship," *Neurological Research* 19 (1997): 1-8.

24. Ibid.

25. Ibid.

26. Kevin Asbjörnson, "The Artistry of Leadership," *Leadership Compass*, no. 10 (2004).

27. Peggy Rostron, "Musician's Tools for the Workplace," New Horizons for Learning, <http://www.newhorizons.org>.

AFTERWORD ENDNOTES

1. Ray Bothamley, "Works in Clay, Creating Sculpture – Stimulating Learning," <http://www.geocities.com/ryanbothamley/>.

2. Joseph Jaworski, Gary Jusela, Claus Otto Scharmer, Dialogue on Leadership, "Coming From Your Inner Self," Conversation with W. Brian Arthur, Xerox Parc, Palo Alto, California, 16 April 1999, <http://www.dialogonleadership.org/Arthur-1999.html>.

APPENDIX ENDNOTES

1. Adapted from Paul Levy, "Using Art in Developing Leadership: Eight Real Examples of Art and Innovation," 2000, <http:www.cats3000.org/Downloads/real.doc>.

The Leader's Brain:

HOW ARE YOU USING THE OTHER 95%

Photo credits:
Page: 2, 22 – Donald Lee, The Banff Centre
Page: 16 – Laurie Buxton, Impression Design
Page: 68,82,114,119,134, 143,156 – Bastiaan Heemsbergen

Book Cover Design:
Laurie Buxton, Impression Design, Canmore, Alberta

For additional information and tools using the H-SAT (Heemsbergen Sensory Awareness Tools), please contact the author at, bastiaan@sympatico.ca or www.drbastiaan.com.

ISBN 141203027-7

9 781412 030274